AUSTRALIAN EXPLORERS
and the places they explored

1860 to 1861: Robert O'Hara Burke and William John Wills started with many others to find a route from Melbourne to the Gulf of Carpentaria. Burke and Wills and two others reached the salt marshes near the Gulf, but only John King survived the trip back.

1770: James Cook and Joseph Banks with 96 officers, crew, marines and civilians in the Endeavour mapped the east coast and collected specimens.

1855 to 1856: Augustus Gregory, an excellent bushman, led the North Australian Expedition from the Victoria River, first to the west, and then east before turning south and travelling to Brisbane, accompanied by botanist Ferdinand von Mueller in a party of 18 men.

1817 and 1818: John Oxley and 12 others first explored the Lachlan and Macquarie valleys, and crossed the Great Dividing Range to Port Macquarie; in 1819, he investigated Jervis Bay and, in 1824, the area around modern Brisbane with Allan Cunningham.

1828 to 1830: Charles Sturt and Hamilton Hume and about a dozen others explored western NSW, reaching the Darling River, and followed the Murrumbidgee and the Murray rivers to the mouth of the Murray by boat; in 1844 to 1846, Sturt and a party of 15 men went from Adelaide through western NSW, seeking a route north, reached the Simpson Desert and almost died.

1789 and 1790: Captain-Lieutenant Watkin Tench, Lieutenant William Dawes and others explored the plains west of Sydney, but could not get past the Blue Mountains.

1798: John Wilson with soldiers and convicts travelled southwest of Sydney.

1795: Matthew Flinders, with George Bass, explored the coastline near Sydney; in 1798, they sailed around Tasmania, proving that it was an island; in 1801 to 1803, Flinders sailed, with five scientists and artists, around Australia's coast, and met Baudin at Encounter Bay.

1813: William Charles Wentworth, Gregory Blaxland and William Lawson, with four servants, found their way from Sydney to the top of the Blue Mountains.

1813 and 1814: George Evans crossed the Blue Mountains with five men and mapped the land on the other side.

Some modern placenames and state and territory borders have been added to this map.

AUSTRALIAN BACKYARD EXPLORER

Peter Macinnis

National Library of Australia

To my granddaughter, Brianna Ng, who mastered the art of walking, the first stage in becoming an explorer, while this book was being written.

Published by the National Library of Australia
Canberra ACT 2600

© National Library of Australia 2009

Every reasonable endeavour has been made to contact the copyright holders. Where this has not been possible, the copyright holders are invited to contact the publisher.

This book is copyright in all countries subscribing to the Berne Convention. Apart from any fair dealing for the purpose of research, criticism or review, as permitted under the *Copyright Act 1968*, no part may be reproduced by any process without written permission. Enquiries should be made to the publisher.

National Library of Australia Cataloguing-in-Publication entry

Author:	Macinnis, P. (Peter)
Title:	Australian backyard explorer / Peter Macinnis.
ISBN:	9780642276841 (pbk.)
Notes:	Includes index.
Target Audience:	For juveniles.
Subjects:	Explorers--Australia--Juvenile literature. Wilderness survival--Australia--Juvenile literature.
Dewey Number:	910.92

Concept Development: Susan Hall

Project Manager:	Joanna Karmel
Editors:	Joanna Karmel and Tina Mattei
Design:	Paul Joice
Illustrations:	Paul Joice
Printer:	Printed in Malaysia for Imago

The National Library of Australia would like to thank Paul Southwell, Joanne Rossiter and the students of Radford College, Canberra, for their comments on the draft of this book.

Front cover images: see pages 46, 52, 53, 61, 107. Thanks to Stephen and Sam Hall for the photo.

Back cover images: see pages 14, 32, 52, 53.

ABOUT THIS BOOK

There are lots of topics that are covered in each chapter. The material is accessible and informative, and has supporting projects, journal entries, 'Did you know?' boxes, 'A closer look' boxes and illustrations.

Journal entries describe explorers' adventures in their own words.

'A closer look' explains a more complicated topic.

Hunting

Wills had also traded with friendly Aboriginal people for some fish in April and May 1861. After the Aboriginal people had left, and not being successful at catching his own fish, he once chased some crows off a fish they'd been eating. At another time, it was only luck that presented him with a meal.

... Having rested a while and eaten a few fish-bones, I moved down the creek, hoping by a late march to be able to reach our own camp; but I soon found, from my extreme weakness, that that would be out of the question. A certain amount of good luck, however, still stuck to me, for on going along by a large waterhole I was so fortunate as to find a large fish, about a pound and a half in weight, which was just being choked by another which it had tried to swallow, but which had stuck in its throat. I soon had a fire lit, and both of the fish cooked and eaten: the large one was in good condition.

William John Wills, 2 June 1861

Mostly, the explorers hunted their meat. In November 1839, John Lort Stokes killed a kangaroo at long range while it was travelling fast. A few days later, he realised that kangaroos which are in a valley always travelled in a curve. They escaped hunters by hopping along the valley before turning slowly up the nearest hill and then going straight up. Stokes would send a man along near the river, while he stayed ahead, well up the hill. As the man by the river startled the kangaroos, they curved up towards Stokes, who shot them at close range.

Admiral John Lort Stokes.

Mounted wallabies posed in lifelike displays in the 1890s.

Bird skins stored in drawers at Museum Victoria.

A Closer Look

Taxidermy

When you last went to a museum, you probably saw dead animals on display. Taxidermy is the art of preserving animal skins to create lifelike animals for display, and someone who does this is called a taxidermist. The word is from the Greek words *taxis*, which means arrangement, and *derma*, which means skin.

Taxidermy became popular in the first half of the nineteenth century when natural history was an exciting new field. Professional and amateur scientists travelled all over the world to collect exotic animals. Their skins were sewn up and stuffed with wood shavings, straw and other material until it looked something like the living animal and then sold to collectors, museums and universities, and also to individuals who just wanted them as curiosities. The animals that were prepared like this were called 'stuffed' animals. The popularity of natural history meant that great numbers of wild animals were slaughtered, many ending up being stuffed. In those days, nobody worried about extinction. Of course, now there are laws that protect many species.

Later in the nineteenth century, the stuffing technique had to change because museums wanted to display specimens that looked much more lifelike. The new techniques, which remain much the same today, included skinning the animal and cutting the head off from the base of the skull. An exact replica of the animal's body was made by either carving balsa wood, or by using fine wood shavings or other fibres. Wire was used for the neck, the tail and the legs. The brain was scooped out of the skull with a small spoon. The skin was then carefully placed around the artificial body and sewn up. Specimens prepared in this way are called 'mounted' specimens.

PROJECT — MAKING A POOTER

A pooter is a neat device that uses suction to pick up small animals safely. It's better than a small brush because the animals are held in a container that's easy to empty into another container.

How to do it:

1. Cut the tubing into a 40-centimetre and a 20-centimetre piece.

2. Remove the lid of the bottle and, with adult help, drill two holes, side by side and fit the tubes.

3. With the lid off wrap and tape two layers of the cloth around the long tube, then pull it back up, so that the filter is near the underside of the lid. Leave the short tube so that it almost reaches the bottom of the bottle. Put the lid back on.

4. Use the glue or sticky tape to hold the tubes in place. You can even use candle wax, but get an adult to help you. If you choose the size of the drill bit carefully, you can probably do without the glue.

5. Find a small insect and put the short tube over it and suck on the long tube to draw it into the pooter. When you have finished looking at the insect, take it back to where you found it and let it go.

put tube close to insect

long tube
fine cloth
short tube

Checklist
- *a small clear plastic bottle*
- *60 cm of plastic tubing (3–4 mm wide)*
- *a drill and a drill bit slightly smaller than the tubing*
- *a small piece of fine cloth*
- *some sticky tape, or some epoxy glue (like Araldite) for a permanent pooter*
- *scissors*

Don't use just a tube as a pooter, or you'll soon learn what it's like to have ...

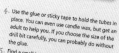

The projects are fun and practical. They have a list of everything you need and step-by-step instructions. Supervision by an adult is recommended.

DID YOU KNOW ?

How would you describe a platypus to someone who has never seen one before? When the first platypus specimen arrived in Britain from Australia in 1799, scientists couldn't believe their eyes. In fact, they thought it was a fraud and that someone was playing a trick on them by sewing pieces of other animals together. Just imagine what they saw—an animal that had a bill like a duck's, a tail like a beaver's and feet like an otter's. To add to its peculiarities, scientists later discovered that the platypus also laid eggs! No other mammal, except the echidna, lays eggs. (An egg-laying mammal is called a monotreme.)

'Did you know?' boxes contain interesting extra facts.

Some strange illustrations of parts of a crocodile, after it'd been killed, from a sketch by Lieutenant Gore of the *Beagle*, 1830s–1840s.

An 'alligator' on the mud, Victoria River, during the Augustus Gregory expedition, 1856. Sometimes, the animals wanted to do the collecting!

Pictures from the National Library of Australia help tell the explorers' stories. You can see these pictures and thousands of others on the Library's website: www.nla.gov.au/digicoll/pictures.html.

CHAPTER 1

WHO WERE THE EXPLORERS?

What's an 'explorer'?

The explorers of the eighteenth and nineteenth centuries were individuals who trekked into areas that they thought were unknown. Some of them went looking for riches, such as land for farming, minerals or timbers—anything that could be sold. Some went looking for interesting places, like high mountains or the fabled inland sea. Others just wanted to find a way to get from one place to another. All of them drew maps.

There are about 40 expedition leaders mentioned in this book. The map on the inside front cover will help you sort out who went where and when.

Ask anybody who the Australian explorers were and most people will be able to mention some of these expedition leaders. That's unfair, because explorers always took others with them, hundreds of followers who are forgotten today, even if their names were sometimes attached to a hill, bay or headland. Who's heard of John Murphy, Euranabie, John Harris, Rose de Freycinet or Tommy Winditj?

The departure of Captain Charles Sturt's expedition, August 1844.

Charles Sturt set out in 1844 with 15 men—including a sailor, a surgeon, a shepherd/butcher and two bullock drivers—30 bullocks, 11 horses, 200 sheep, four kangaroo dogs and two sheep dogs. Sir Thomas Mitchell took 30 men in 1845, including a shoemaker, a blacksmith, eight bullock drivers, two carpenters, two mounted soldiers and a barometer-carrier. There were a lot more explorers than the ones who appear in the history books.

Forgotten explorers

Behind every famous explorer there were tough survivors, people who knew how to handle animals; hunt and kill for food; mend equipment, clothes and broken bones; climb cliffs and mountains; hack paths and make bridges; and more. Some of them, like Allan Cunningham, John McDouall Stuart and Edmund Kennedy, became famous later, but most of them did not.

Even some of the leaders miss out on recognition. Who's heard of John Wilson, George Evans, James Grant, Herschel Babbage or John Horrocks? One way or another, they were all explorers, but we've forgotten many more of them than we remember.

In 1817, John Oxley set off along the Macquarie River in New South Wales. He took George Evans as second-in-command, two botanists, a mineralogist, surgeon John Harris, a boat-builder, a boatman, a horse-shoer, a butcher, a horse leader, a harness mender, a chainman to help in surveys, and a servant.

Later in the year, when Lieutenant Phillip Parker King went to map the Australian coast in the cutter *Mermaid*, he took two experienced seamen who could manage the vessel, 12 other seamen, two boys and Allan Cunningham, one of Oxley's botanists. John Septimus Roe, one of the experienced seamen, later became famous as an explorer, like Cunningham, but the rest have been forgotten.

An explorer camping out for the night. The tent is large enough to hold six men, yet only one man is shown, and one horse. The cooking pot would be too large to carry on a horse, but where is the dray or cart and the horses to pull it? Where are the other explorers?

A statue of John Septimus Roe, surveyor and explorer, Perth.

Convict explorers

The First Fleet of 11 ships sailed from England in May 1787, reaching Botany Bay in January 1788. Finding the area unsuitable for a permanent settlement, Governor Arthur Phillip left the fleet and sailed out of Botany Bay in search of a more suitable place. Soon after he left, two French ships, commanded by La Pérouse, entered Botany Bay and set up camp on the shore. On the same day, the remaining ships of the First Fleet left the bay and followed Phillip to Port Jackson (now Sydney Harbour), landing at Sydney Cove. This was the beginning of the city of Sydney.

There were 729 convicts among those who travelled with the First Fleet. Within a few days of arriving at Sydney Cove, some of the convicts discovered the 'road to Botany Bay'—a track made by the Eora people, the Aboriginal inhabitants of the area. On reaching Botany Bay, the convicts asked the French to take them back to Europe. The French refused, but three of them followed the same track back to Sydney, where they were greeted with surprise by Governor Phillip and his officers.

The 24th, in the morning, two strange ships were discover'd to ye southward of Cape Solander, and we soon after discover'd that they were French, one of which wore a chef d'escadre's pennant, from which we conclude them to be La Boussole and L'Astrolabe, under ye orders of Monsieur de La Perouse, on discoveries, but the wind blowing strong from N. N. E. prevented their getting in or our going out.

Philip Gidley King, 24 January 1788

The Frenchmen came with guns, as if they were hunting. The British suspected they were actually interested in spying on the new settlement, but the governor was polite, and sent two horses over the track to bring La Pérouse from Botany Bay to Sydney. So, the first explorers on land after the First Fleet came ashore were some unnamed convicts and then some unnamed Frenchmen.

By 1798, many convicts believed in a mythical settlement of white people, three to four hundred miles (around 600 kilometres) south-west of Sydney. To reach there, escapers would have to get through the rugged Snowy Mountains and into eastern Victoria, somewhere between Albury, Shepparton, Sale and Mallacoota. Nobody knew the country, but there were still 'maps' being passed around, which supposedly showed how to reach this paradise.

Governor John Hunter was worried that many convicts might perish in the bush, trying to reach this mythical place. He decided to send John (or James) Wilson, who was a capable convict bushman, out with an expedition of convicts and soldiers, towards the 'settlement'. The idea was to let the convicts see how dreadful the country was, before Wilson brought them safely back again.

The convicts had other ideas and planned for a strong group to follow the party. Their idea was to steal the soldiers' weapons and push on for the fabled white settlement. But, their plot was uncovered, the ringleaders were delayed and extra soldiers were added to the party.

The soldiers took the convicts out a long way, then they turned back to Sydney without them. Three of the convicts were allowed to go with them

Henry Angel was one of six convicts who accompanied Hamilton Hume and William Hovell on their exploration trip to Port Phillip.

because they were already worn out. Wilson led the rest into Sydney two weeks later. After that, the convicts gave up taking off into the bush to find the mythical white settlement, but they did still go wandering, closer to home.

Convicts were often listed in explorers' reports just as 'servants', although Ludwig Leichhardt was more blunt when he described his 1844–1846 team, calling team member William Phillips 'a prisoner of the crown'. Phillips had the habit of always setting up his tent away from the others, perhaps because he was a convict.

The early convicts were not locked up in cells, so they could move around, even if there were guards to stop them going too far. Some of the convicts quickly learned their way around the bush and avoided the guards when they wanted to. Wilson started living with the local Aborigines, who taught him bushcraft, accepted him and made him an initiated man.

Hamilton Hume and William Hovell each took three convicts on their expedition from near Yass, New South Wales, to Port Phillip, near modern Geelong in Victoria. Hume's men included Henry Angel, who had been working as a farmhand on Hume's property. Angel managed the working horses and cattle, and planned the transport for the expedition. He and two other convicts were the first Europeans to swim across the Murray River. After the expedition, Hovell did nothing for his convict servants, who remained servants. On the other hand, Hume rewarded Angel and his two other convict servants by getting them tickets-of-leave, which meant that they could get their own jobs, even though they were still convicts, rather than being given a job by the government. Angel later became a free man and bought his own land.

A map showing what '300 to 400 miles southwest of Sydney' meant: passing the area where Canberra is now and then Mount Kosciuszko, crossing the Snowy Mountains and on into eastern Victoria.

(inset) Hamilton Hume and William Hovell setting out on their expedition in 1824. We know the names of the six convicts they took with them. An Aboriginal man was also part of the expedition but we don't know his name.

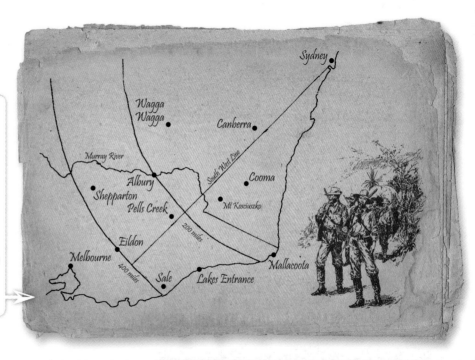

A breastplate given by Governor Sir Charles Fitzroy to Jackey Jackey, Aboriginal servant to the explorer Edmund Kennedy.

Aboriginal explorers

Leichhardt's team also included John Murphy, 'a lad of about 16 years old' and Harry Brown, who was 'an aboriginal of the Newcastle tribe'. Teenagers and Aboriginal men were common on expeditions. Boys did as they were told, fetching wood and water and doing other hard and boring tasks. Aboriginal men served as guides and hunters, and were also used to negotiate with any Aboriginal tribes that an expedition might come across.

At first, Sydney Aboriginal people, like Euranabie and his wife Worogan, or Bungaree or Bundell, were taken along on sea voyages so they could 'speak to the Indians'. With time, explorers came to realise that there were many Aboriginal languages, so they took their Aboriginal companions along more as proof that they came with peaceful intentions, and for their bush skills in tracking an expedition's animals. Even though two of a horse's or a camel's legs were tied together (or hobbled) to stop it wandering, the animal could travel a long way during the night.

Only three Aboriginal people appear regularly in the history books: Bungaree who sailed on many trips, Wylie who accompanied John Eyre around

An explorer and an Aboriginal guide, about 1850.

Bungaree, chief of the Broken Bay tribe, New South Wales, joined the ships, the *Norfolk*, the *Lady Nelson*, the *Investigator* and the *Mermaid*, on four trips between 1799 and 1817, circumnavigating Australia.

the Great Australian Bight, and Jackey Jackey who travelled with Kennedy on his fatal trip towards Cape York. But many other exploring parties only made it back because they had Aboriginal people along to help. John and Alexander Forrest were expert navigators, but they needed Tommy Winditj to find water and feed for the horses. When he died, they paid for his headstone, on which was written that he was 'an aboriginal native of Western Australia of great intelligence and fidelity'.

William Landsborough with the Aboriginal members of his party, Jemmy and Jacky, about 1862. At this time, photographs were rare.

John Eyre and Wylie, his Aboriginal companion, struggling along a beach on the Great Australian Bight.

Occasionally, Sturt's men had problems when Aboriginal people swam out and grabbed their oars.

John Forrest, explorer of Western Australia.

John Forrest's party (his brother, Alexander, was second-in-command) sight the Overland Telegraph Line, 1874.

Governor explorers and women explorers

Even a few governors went exploring. In Western Australia, Governor FitzGerald was speared in the leg, just above his knee, in 1848, not far from today's Geraldton, and Sir Richard MacDonnell, the Governor of South Australia, made a long expedition into the dry outback in 1859. Governor Macquarie's trips in New South Wales around 1815 were more like tourist trips but, in Tasmania, Sir John and Lady Franklin took real risks when they visited the west coast in 1838.

In South Australia in 1839, Governor George Gawler and Captain Sturt went up the Murray River by boat. They took along Mrs Sturt, Julia Gawler, the governor's teenage daughter, her teenage maid, Eliza Arbuckle and an English boy of 18, Henry Bryan. It may sound like a pleasant river cruise but, before it ended, Henry Bryan became lost and disappeared without trace, confused in a strange land.

Rose de Freycinet also disappeared without trace, but only from the official records. She stowed away on her husband's ship, the *Uranie*, and travelled the world with him for three years, including on a long survey of the Australian coast. She was never officially mentioned in Freycinet's account, though he and his crew named a dove and an island after her. She appeared in a watercolour that was painted on the voyage, but when the painting was later engraved for printing, Rose de Freycinet was removed. This was because French Government officials disapproved of her presence on the *Uranie*, as women were forbidden from boarding government ships.

A young girl stowed away on Phillip Parker King's 1821 voyage in the brig *Bathurst*, because she loved one of the officers. The crew found her dreadfully seasick in the hold after three days, but it was too late for the vessel to turn back, so she stayed on the boat for almost 11 months. Her name and any details of her later life have vanished.

Sir John Franklin, Governor of Tasmania and explorer.

We set off in beautiful weather, and in a season of unusually prolonged drought, but had scarcely commenced it, when the rains came on which made the bogs in a shocking state, and flooded all the torrents and rivers. We were confined a week in our tents in a nook under a snowy mountain, and again were impeded by a wide impetuous river which the surveyor had called the Franklin. It was 70 or 80 yards wide, too wide for any fallen trees to cross it, as we had crossed all the others, and where in consequence the pioneering party had constructed a rude kind of raft which they had fastened by a rope across the River. On our arrival the flood had carried away the warp, but the raft remained; on this after the river had subsided a little, two men, (prisoners) volunteered to cross.

Lady Franklin, April 1842

The case of the disappearing Rose. You can see Rose de Freycinet in front of the tall tent in the original watercolour (bottom), but she has been removed in the engraved version (top).

What other differences can you spot?

CHAPTER 2

FINDING A WAY AND LEAVING SIGNS

Aboriginal people were often shown as a threat in nineteenth-century images. Here, Charles Sturt's party is facing the local people at the junction of the Murray and Darling rivers in 1830. Sturt always succeeded in making a peaceful settlement.

We often think of explorers as brave men who ventured into a wilderness where nobody had ever been. But it's a myth that the land was empty of people. Aboriginal people had been living in Australia for over 40 000 years and explorers knew of their existence. One of the explorers' greatest fears was that they might be attacked but, although there were Aboriginal warriors who did object to the trespassers in their country, in many cases the Aboriginal people were friendly and helpful.

Aboriginal people about to attack Ludwig Leichhardt's camp near the Gulf of Carpentaria in 1845. This image ignores the many peaceful and friendly contacts Leichhardt had with Aboriginal people. Some say that the attack was revenge for one of Leichhardt's party assaulting an Aboriginal woman.

Using Aboriginal pathways

Even before the first Europeans arrived at Port Jackson (now Sydney) in 1788, Arthur Bowes Smyth, the surgeon from the convict ship, the *Lady Penrhyn,* mentioned seeing 'cat paths' at Botany Bay. These paths were foot tracks that, later, led some convict wanderers over to Botany Bay.

When you read the journals of the explorers, they often refer to following tracks. They knew that they'd been made by Aboriginal people even if they didn't always see these people. In Western Port, Victoria, in April 1801, James Grant reported seeing 'many natives' paths and marks of fires', but saw none of the people who had made them. In 1841, Edward John Eyre was in harsh country, but he knew which way to go when he found a 'native pathway'.

Aboriginal tracks were often referred to as 'native paths', though Eyre sometimes called them 'native roads'. In those days, any path that you could travel along, even if it were just a track through the scrub, might be called a road. Ludwig Leichhardt followed a 'well beaten foot-path of the natives' in September 1845 and 'a broad foot-path of the natives' in October. In November, Charles Sturt followed 'a large path, crossing numerous small branches of the creek with deep and sandy beds, and occasionally over small stony plains'. According to John Wills' notes, dated 10 February 1861, his party managed to find 'a path formed by the blacks'. Using the path was better than wandering through the scrub, he said, because the ground was well-trodden and hard.

One of the oldest exploration myths was that Gregory Blaxland, William Charles Wentworth and William Lawson were brilliant because they worked out that the way over the Blue Mountains west of Sydney was to 'follow the ridges' at the top of the mountains. But how did they get to these ridges? They had the sense to use existing paths that went up the spurs—nice easy slopes that work up to the top. The paths were Aboriginal tracks that had been walked for thousands of years. The true cleverness of Blaxland, Wentworth and Lawson was that they realised that if they followed these Aboriginal tracks, they would end up somewhere.

Edward John Eyre was always sympathetic towards Aboriginal people. In 1840, when he heard about the spearing of a white boy in South Australia, he could understand why it had happened. From the Aboriginal people's point of view, Europeans were in their country, uninvited.

... our being in their country at all is, so far as their ideas of right and wrong are concerned, altogether an act of intrusion and aggression ... our presence and settlement, in any particular locality, do, in point of fact, actually dispossess the aboriginal inhabitants.

Edward John Eyre, 6 October 1840

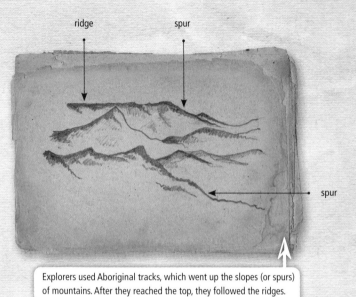

ridge   spur

spur

Explorers used Aboriginal tracks, which went up the slopes (or spurs) of mountains. After they reached the top, they followed the ridges.

Port Jackson (left) and Govetts Leap, the Blue Mountains (below). Imagine finding your way up or down these cliffs.

Exploring off the track in dry country

Explorers often made bad choices when they went out into places they didn't know, straying into deserts, pushing into swamps, venturing into ravines or almost falling over cliffs. Big problems arose when there were no tracks.

In dry country, explorers got into difficulties when they tried to conquer sand dunes that ran for hundreds of kilometres. Sturt was an experienced bushman when he set off to cross dune country in late 1844. He found his way blocked by sand ridges 'thirty to fifty feet high, and about eighty yards at their base' (10 to 15 metres high and about 70 metres across). Although there were plants on the dunes, the sand was still soft and hard to climb.

Wind blows dry sand up a dune where it piles up until it can't pile up anymore. The slope at this point is called the angle of rest and, if more sand is blown up the slope, the whole side slides down, making a new base onto which sand is blown until the same thing happens again.

Climbing sand dunes exhausted and depressed the explorers because whenever they or their animals stepped onto a dune, the sand would come tumbling down the slope and each foothold would slide down. That is why climbing a 15-metre dune needs the same energy as climbing a 50-metre staircase.

Denison Ranges, central Australia. Clear animal tracks like these are formed over time. Animals know the easiest ways to go, so when people find their tracks, they follow them.

PROJECT   THE SAND DUNE ANGLE

The wind blows more and more sand onto a sand dune until it reaches a point where no more sand can be added without the sand slipping down the sides. The angle of the side of the dune at this point is called the angle of rest.

To see how sand dunes form this steep angle, all you need is a bucket and some dry sand. It can be a bit messy, so this is a good thing to try at the beach, somewhere well away from the water, where the top layers of sand have dried in the sun.

Wind blows sand up the sand dune.

How to do it:

1. Scrape a nice flat area to work on.
2. Fill your bucket about half-full with warm dry sand, avoiding sticks and leaves.
3. Tilt the bucket and start pouring sand onto one spot. As a cone builds up, keep pouring sand onto its tip, and see how the sand slides down and then starts building up on the most recent slide. The trick is to pour slowly and gently.

What else you can do:

Compare the angle of rest for other substances, such as grains of rice, sugar, flour, polenta or macaroni.

34° = angle of rest

Checklist
- a beach with plenty of dry sand
- a small bucket

A man struggling up a sand dune in mid-north South Australia.

To explorers, high sand was a great enemy, but low sand was a different sort of enemy. When thirsty explorers dug a hole in a sandy riverbed to reach water, the sides would collapse in. The deeper they dug, the wider the hole had to be at the top, to keep the sides from falling in. Each time a human or an animal went down the slope to get water, the sand would tumble down and it would have to be dug out again.

A wall of sand suddenly rose before us, such as we had not before seen; lying as it did directly across our course we had no choice but to ascend. For 20 miles we toiled over as distressing a country as can be imagined, each succeeding sand ridge assumed a steeper and more rugged character, and the horse with difficulty pulled the cart along.

Charles Sturt, 24 August 1845

An aerial view of parallel sand dunes in the desert in north-east South Australia.

Cutting through thick bush

For the explorers, thick bush was far worse than open and sandy country. Aboriginal people walked along their paths often enough to keep them open, but any explorer who strayed from a track or missed it could be in all sorts of trouble. Trees and branches made a barrier that explorers had to cut through and that their animals had to force a way through. Hacking trees every few metres left sharp and jagged pieces sticking out, often ripping the men's bags, clothes and flesh, and the animals' harnesses and bodies.

Flour was one of the main types of food that the explorers thought they couldn't do without. They carried it in huge quantities in bags but, unless the bags were well-protected, they would be ripped open by rocks or trees, spilling the flour onto the ground. Other important items, such as delicate instruments like barometers, might be lost when explorers hacked through the bush. In the end, explorers had to be self-sufficient. They had to take the stores they needed, such as axles for carts, clothes and animal harnesses, and anything else had to be made on the way or repaired. It was either that or go without.

Depending on the type of country, many explorers preferred travelling at night when the moon was up, especially in summer, but others, like Giles, found that this was risky.

The desert in central Australia is a harsh place.

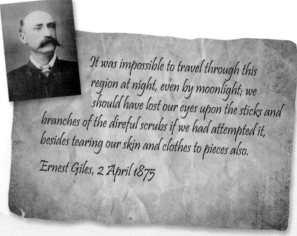

It was impossible to travel through this region at night, even by moonlight; we should have lost our eyes upon the sticks and branches of the direful scrubs if we had attempted it, besides tearing our skin and clothes to pieces also.

Ernest Giles, 2 April 1875

In this painting by S.T. Gill, John Horrocks and Gill are inspecting the countryside in South Australia in 1846. It looks as if Horrocks is comparing Gill's landscape painting with the scene below them.

DID YOU KNOW ?

CAMEL TEAM IN FLOODED COUNTRY.
SOUTH AUST.

Camels were brought to Australia from India to carry supplies specifically
for the Burke and Wills expedition. Camels are adapted to living in deserts
—their feet have elastic but tough soles that prevent them from sinking into
the sand, hair on the head and hump that regulates their body temperature, and a hump
that stores food for when they need it. They can survive for up to five weeks without food
and for four to six days without water. They can get water from the food they eat and they
can drink water that is too salty for other animals.

Ferns in the Dandenongs, Victoria, about 1880. Some
explorers had to hack their way through forests like this.

Trekking along the beach

You might think that using beaches as pathways would be a good choice for expeditions but, in many cases, it was very unwise. In Western Australia, in 1839, George Grey's party walked along the north coast, taking little water because it was confidently expecting to find a giant river. Unfortunately, there was no river and Grey and his companions could easily have died of thirst. On the southern coast of Western Australia, Eyre was luckier, as he found fresh water in the sand dunes at the back of some beaches. He also met up with a boat carrying supplies for his party and, later, by chance, with some whalers who probably saved his life.

In 1818, when John Oxley and his party walked along the beaches from Port Macquarie towards Newcastle in New South Wales, they faced problems when they came to rivers. They had plenty of fresh water, but no boat to move their stores from one side of a river to the other. On a beach, they found a boat partly buried in the sand, which had come from a wrecked ship. When they came across their first river, 12 of the men trudged 20 kilometres back to the boat and carried it 20 kilometres back to the river. They were so pleased with it that they carried it on to Port Stephens. Later, a small group from Oxley's party used the boat to reach Newcastle and get help.

Hamilton Hume and William Hovell were very inventive when they came to a flooded Murrumbidgee River: they took the wheels off a cart, wrapped it in a tarpaulin to make it waterproof, and used it as a boat.

Eyre's party farewell the men from the supply boat during their overland crossing from Adelaide, west along the coast. After this point, there were no places where a boat could land until they had passed from South Australia into Western Australia.

Hamilton Hume and William Hovell crossing the Murrumbidgee in 1824 in a boat made out of a cart and a tarpaulin.

...er comes to Eyre's aid, Great Australian Bight, 1841.

Hume and Hovell crossing the Murray in 1825, a long time before there were bridges.

Here, in the Great Australian Bight, in 1841, Eyre was lucky enough to be seen by the *Mississippi*, a French whaler. Eyre's health was bad and his food rations were low, but a stay with the whalers got him on his feet again. In this picture, he is greeting Captain Rossiter from the whaler. Wylie, Eyre's Aboriginal companion, is in the background with the horses.

PROJECT MAKING A LAUNDRY BASKET BOAT

The explorers could waterproof almost anything by wrapping it in a tarpaulin (or tarp), which was a canvas sheet treated with tar to stop water soaking through it. In this project, you'll do something like this by trying to stop a laundry basket from leaking using a light modern plastic, such as blue polytarp, to replace the tarpaulin. As the name suggests, a polytarp is a modern type of tarpaulin made from a plastic called polyethylene.

How to do it:

Clip or tie the sheeting in place to make the laundry basket waterproof. Your boat won't be very stable, so you need adult supervision during the testing stage, and you need to be able to swim. Test it in shallow water, away from any hard rocks or pool edges that you might hurt yourself on.

Checklist
- a plastic laundry basket
- some waterproof sheeting (plastic or blue polytarp)
- safe shallow water (a pool or sandy beach)
- some bulldog clips or rope to hold the sheeting in place
- a paddle of some sort (if your boat works)

Rising in the world

If explorers wanted to see what lay ahead, they climbed a tree, a hill or, best of all, a mountain. On his expedition along the Macquarie River, John Oxley climbed a small rise that he named Mount Harris. It probably took him ten minutes to stroll up this hill, which he estimated was just 'two to three hundred feet' high but, from the top, he could see the mountains called the Warrumbungles. Oxley headed for them. When he got there, he set off up Mount Exmouth, which he succeeded climbing after 'nearly two hours of hard labour to ascend its rugged summits'.

In 2006, I walked up Mount Exmouth along a good track and it still took me well over three hours. So, for Oxley to take less than two hours, he must have been following a clear track that had been made by Aboriginal people.

From the top of Mount Exmouth, Oxley could see part of the Great Dividing Range, so he headed for that, climbed it, and then descended almost 1000 metres to Port Macquarie in September 1818. I saw what he saw as a distant smudge in the haze, but I took his word that the Great Dividing Range was there and drove along the highway that more or less follows his route. Today, as we drive along a highway, we can go further in a car in one hour than an explorer could go in one week of hard slog.

A cairn on Mount Harris that was probably built on top of one that had been left by Oxley's party. (A cairn is a pile of stones set up as a monument.)

A view of the Warrumbungles.

A Closer Look

How did explorers estimate the heights of mountains?

All the explorers, like Oxley, estimated the heights of the mountains they climbed. Sometimes they did this by using barometers to measure the air pressure, which gets less as you go up. However, barometers were hard to carry, so sometimes they boiled water and measured the boiling point, which drops as the air pressure gets less (and air pressure gets less as you're climbing the mountain). In 1844, Charles Sturt took a barometer and two thermometers so he could measure the boiling point.

At sea level, water boils at 100°C. A rise of 280 metres lowers the boiling point by 1°C. This means that an accurate thermometer could detect a difference of about 30 metres, which was good enough for most estimations of height. The problem was that air pressure (and therefore the boiling point of water) varies with the weather, so there was always a bit of uncertainty.

Ernest Giles climbed Mount Conner, not far from Uluru, in 1873. He took, as he described it, 'all the apparatus necessary for so great an ascent': thermometer, barometer, compass, field glasses, quart pot (a pot that can contain a little over one litre), waterbag and matches. Unfortunately, the barometer was damaged during the climb. So, he measured the boiling point and got 206°F (97°C), which he converted to 'an elevation of 3085 feet [940 metres] above the level of the sea, it being about 1200 feet [366 metres] above the surrounding country'. Today, with more accurate ways of measuring, we know it is 859 metres above sea level and 300 metres above the plain.

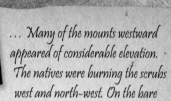

... Many of the mounts westward appeared of considerable elevation. The natives were burning the scrubs west and north-west. On the bare rocks of this mountain we saw several white, bleached snail-shells. I was grieved to find that my barometer had met with an accident in our climb; however, by testing the boiling point of water I obtained the altitude.

Water boiled at 206 degrees, giving an elevation of 3085 feet above the level of the sea, it being about 1200 feet above the surrounding country.

Ernest Giles, 30 August 1873

A view of Mount Kosciuszko, the highest mountain in Australia. Eugene von Guérard produced this hand-coloured lithograph, called *Mount Kosciusko, from the North-west*, in 1867.

John McDouall Stuart raises the British flag on what he called 'Central Mount Sturt', a name that was later changed to 'Central Mount Stuart', in the centre of Australia.

Leaving marks behind

When explorers hacked their way through scrub, they carved words and numbers on trees. (If you did this now, you'd be called a vandal!) They also left other signs, many of which lasted for a long time, especially in the drier parts of Australia, such as the ruts that wheels of carts had made. Where the bush was thicker, the marks of axes and saws showed where the party had cleared 'a road' for drays, carts or animals. These signs could last for decades.

In 1819, Lieutenant Phillip Parker King took John Oxley back to Port Macquarie, arriving by sea, rather than by travelling over the Great Dividing Range as Oxley had done on his first visit, eight months earlier. They went ashore and noticed that the signs of Oxley's earlier visit were disappearing, but they could still see axe marks along the river banks, where Oxley's party had cleared a way. On the trek through the mountains, Oxley's men had eventually abandoned anything with wheels, putting their supplies on horses.

To cope with their loads, most explorers at least started out with carts, drays or wagons, and horses, camels or bullocks. A person can only carry about 25 kilograms on long trips, but a packhorse can manage about 150 kilograms, a camel can carry around 300 kilograms, and a horse can pull a cart carrying up to 450 kilograms over level ground. Pack bullocks could carry on their backs about the same weight as horses could. The explorers' animals left droppings and footprints behind. These signs of their presence remained for a year or more, while the carts left wheel ruts that lasted a lot longer.

Charles Sturt and his party at Depot Creek. Note the number of men, the guns, the wooden buckets, the cart and the horses. Explorers like Sturt knew what they needed to take.

This medal, a breastplate, was made to thank the Yandruwandha people for helping Burke, Wills and King. It says: 'Presented by the Exploration Committee of Victoria for the Humanity shewn [shown] to the Explorers Burke, Wills & King 1861'. Breastplates were worn around the neck.

People in the bush learned to read the tracks and signs and, when Alfred Howitt was searching for the lost members of the Burke and Wills' party on 15 September 1861, he read the signs clearly. He could see that there had been two horses feeding near a large waterhole, and he also found the handle of a clasp knife (a knife with a blade that folds into the handle, like a penknife). Nearby, he saw a camel's track and droppings on a 'native path'. The camel's footprint was about four months old and going east, he said.

Other signs that explorers left behind included the bones of slaughtered sheep, cattle, horses, camels or goats, as well as old fireplaces, cuts made on trees and lost items like the clasp knife handle. Some relics disappeared because Aboriginal people picked them up for their own use—a cast horseshoe made a fine axe, a tent peg became a perfect digging-stick, and pieces of glass could be made into spearheads and sharp blades.

Today, there are relic-hunters who search for items from past expeditions. In 2001, two brothers from Adelaide came across a brass medal while on a fishing trip to Cooper Creek. Their curiosity about the item soon turned into great excitement when they realised what they had found—a medal that had been made especially for the Aboriginal people who had looked after Robert O'Hara Burke, William John Wills and John King in 1861. For six years, the brothers kept their discovery to themselves until they decided to sell the medal. But the South Australian Government thought the medal was such an important part of our history that it said that it could only be sold as long as it stayed in South Australia and could be seen by the public. It was sold for $180 000 in April 2008 and presented to the South Australian Museum. There are two more medals still out there somewhere. You could look for them yourself but you'd have to go to the Simpson Desert, which is a very remote and hostile place in South Australia's far north.

Soon after the sale of the medal, a Melbourne man found some more relics from one of the Burke and Wills' camps, including a rifle, a revolver, bullets, a spirit level (an instrument for measuring whether something is horizontal), buckles, a sewing kit, hinges and latches. Using Wills' notes and modern techniques, he'd worked out the location of this particular camp over 20 years earlier.

A tree in Queensland marked by Ludwig Leichhardt during his expedition north from the Darling Downs to Port Essington in 1844–1846.

Leaving messages

Many of the explorers left notes sealed in bottles for later explorers. John Oxley left one near today's town of Booligal, New South Wales, in 1817, but it was lost when the bottle was smashed. Either someone watched it being buried and wanted the glass to make spearheads, or somebody saw where the hole had been filled in and wanted to find out what was inside.

Bottles on islands lasted longer. When Lieutenant King was at King George's Sound (now Albany, Western Australia) in 1822, he rowed out to an island to retrieve a bottle he'd left there in 1818. It was still there, so he took it on board the ship to add some extra information for sailors, and then put it back again. In his notes, he wrote that the locals were friendly and he listed some words from their language.

Often explorers marked the trunks or large branches of trees. These marks were either messages for other parties or they were the explorers' initials and dates to show that they'd been at that place. Some markings on trees have been damaged by fire or the trees' bark has grown over them, but some marks have lasted.

Charles Sturt's marked tree, 'Sturt 1845', Cooper Creek, South Australia.

There are a number of famous marked trees. Augustus Gregory, delayed by a mare giving birth during the North Australian Expedition's trip, carved 'NAE, 11 Jan 1856' on a large gum tree. The old explorers used Roman numbers because they are mainly straight lines, which are easy to carve with a few chops of an axe. In April 1861, William Brahe, who'd been waiting for four months at a camp, Camp 65, on Cooper Creek for Burke and Wills' party to return, carved three messages on a gum tree indicating where he'd buried food, the number of the camp and the dates of arrival and departure. This tree is the most famous of all the marked trees and is called the Dig Tree.

The Dig Tree at Burke and Wills' camp, Camp 65, on Cooper Creek. The marks on the branch, 'DEC 6–60' and 'APR 21–61', are the dates of the expedition's arrival and of Brahe's departure from the camp. The marks on the trunk, 'DIG under' and an arrow, indicate where food had been buried.

CHAPTER 3

FOOD

Carrying food

Choosing what and how much to take into the bush is always a challenge. A fit adult bushwalker can carry about 20 kilograms (about the weight of a six-year-old) and a super-fit walker might manage 30 kilograms (about the weight of a nine-year-old), but that is pretty much the limit. A bushwalker needs about a kilogram of food each day.

There's a lot of water in food. To make food weigh less, the water can be removed and the food becomes dried food. Packet soup is an example of this: just add hot water to the dry ingredients in a mug and it becomes soup. Bushwalkers often take dried food with them, but even dried food for one person for a day will weigh at least 500 grams.

Explorers who travelled long distances couldn't carry enough food on their backs, so they took along pack animals and carts, as well as guns and ammunition to kill food along the way. Some explorers even took herds of sheep and cattle to have a supply of fresh meat. Charles Sturt and his party set out in 1844 with 11 horses, 30 bullocks, 200 sheep, four kangaroo dogs and two sheep dogs. Robert O'Hara Burke and William John Wills' expedition party departed Melbourne in 1860; there were 19 people, 26 camels, 23 horses, six wagons and 20 tonnes of stores.

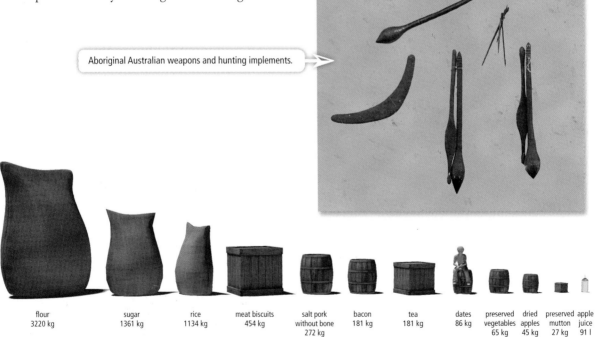

Aboriginal Australian weapons and hunting implements.

| flour 3220 kg | sugar 1361 kg | rice 1134 kg | meat biscuits 454 kg | salt pork without bone 272 kg | bacon 181 kg | tea 181 kg | dates 86 kg | preserved vegetables 65 kg | dried apples 45 kg | preserved mutton 27 kg | apple juice 91 l |

These containers represent some of the stores that the Burke and Wills' expedition took with it. To give an idea of the amounts, the nine-year-old boy on the barrel of dates weighs 30 kilograms.

DID YOU KNOW ?

Scurvy!

healthy

sick with scurvy

Imagine getting a disease like scurvy!

A couple of hundred years ago, members of expeditions (especially sailors and others on ships) often suffered from scurvy when supplies of fresh fruit and vegetables ran out. Many died from this disease.

Why?

Because no fruit and vegetables means no vitamin C. And no vitamin C means scurvy.

The good news was that you could get better—as long as it didn't kill you first!

How do you think you could become healthy again?

VH-UPV

Mrs Lores Bonney checking *My Little Ship*, a DH 60G Moth, after arriving in Darwin on 11 April 1933.

Learning about bush tucker

Some explorers were able to get advice about bush tucker from Aboriginal members of their parties but, because there were hundreds of different Aboriginal groups each with its own territory and language, once the Aboriginal guides were out of their home country, they didn't know about the local food, and the party began to stray into danger. For the explorers, there were no shops selling whatever they forgot, so every choice involved risk. Leave something out and they could die; carry it and they might slow themselves down so that they died anyhow. Carry the wrong food and they could get scurvy, a disease caused by not getting enough vitamin C in their diet.

In the late 1980s, I took a pioneer Australian aviator, Mrs Lores Bonney, on a night visit around the museum where I worked. She was in her nineties and agreed to ride in a wheelchair through the collections. She was one of Australia's last explorer–adventurers, flying around the continent in 1932. For two hours, we chatted about her adventures. I learned that she'd done what the more successful explorers had done. As she'd planned to follow the coast, she talked to coastal Aboriginal people of northern Australia about bush tucker because she knew she would need it if her plane failed.

Many explorers were fascinated, from a scientific point of view, by the plants and animals they saw on their journeys, describing them in detail and sometimes drawing them in their journals. Others accepted bush tucker from the Aboriginal people who lived in the area, sometimes out of politeness and sometimes when they were running out of their own supplies. For some, learning about bush food meant the difference between life and death. On his expedition into central Australia in 1845, Charles Sturt was suffering from scurvy. After seeing local Aboriginal people eating small berries, Mr Browne, a member of Sturt's party, collected a large dishful. Sturt believed that these berries, which were full of vitamin C, were the reason why he recovered from his illness.

These 'pea' plants, *Gompholobium grandiflorum* (far left) and *Gastrolobium calycinum* (left), have the toxin, sodium fluoroacetate, in their leaf tips and seeds.

Poisonous plants

Animals can flee from attackers but plants cannot, so many of them have evolved chemical defences that make them poisonous. The seeds of many of the native 'pea' plants, for example, contain a chemical called sodium fluoroacetate, which is toxic to people and livestock, as some of the explorers discovered. Today, sodium fluoroacetate is put in a product that farmers use to kill pests, like foxes and wild dogs.

Australia's marsupial mammals are fairly immune to plant poisons (or they avoid the plants), but camels, sheep and horses can all be harmed by eating these plants. Ernest Giles noted that shepherds on sheep stations were expected to know all the poisonous plants in their area and to keep the sheep away from them. Camels, on the other hand, have long necks and can bite a lump from any plant, poisonous or not, as they stride along.

Humans can eat poisonous cycad and pandanus seeds but only after they've been treated to get rid of the poisons. The explorers discovered how to treat poisonous plants by examining food left behind when the Aboriginal inhabitants fled their camps at the sight of the strange white invaders.

Aboriginal people smoking out possums (top) and hunting kangaroos (above and below).

Pandanus fruit.

A cycad palm with an empty seed cone.

Members of Ludwig Leichhardt's party tried pandanus seeds in September 1845 and became ill, yet pandanus seeds seemed to be one of the main foods of the local Aboriginal people in that season.

By looking around a deserted Aboriginal camp and seeing food in various stages of preparation, Leichhardt worked out that the people made the seeds safe to eat by roasting them in ashes, soaking and slicing them, and then roasting them on hot stones, but the fine details were still unclear to him. All the same, explorers knew they needed to eat fresh plants. Their ideas on scurvy were confused, but just about everybody agreed that this disease was prevented by eating plants of some sort.

In 1858, John McDouall Stuart was out in dry country in South Australia where he ate pigface and sow-thistle, plants he declared to be 'very palatable' and 'very good'. Burke and Wills ate a kind of damper, given to them by the local Aboriginal people, made from the ground spore pods of the nardoo fern. There was plenty of nardoo in the area but, when Wills prepared it, he was puzzled why it didn't do him any good; yet it was nutritious for the Aboriginal people.

The Aboriginal people knew from long experience that they had to rinse nardoo flour well and roast it before eating it, otherwise it would poison them. What Wills didn't know was that nardoo contained a dangerous chemical. So when Wills didn't prepare it in the same way as the Aboriginal people, he and Burke suffered a disease called beriberi, caused by the dangerous nardoo chemical. They died. Nobody can say for sure what killed them, but it was probably a combination of illnesses caused by bad diet, including beriberi and scurvy.

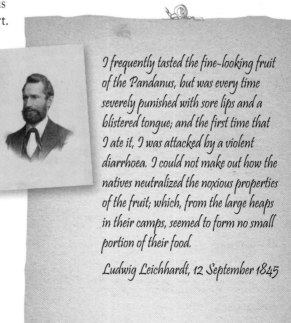

I frequently tasted the fine-looking fruit of the Pandanus, but was every time severely punished with sore lips and a blistered tongue; and the first time that I ate it, I was attacked by a violent diarrhoea. I could not make out how the natives neutralized the noxious properties of the fruit; which, from the large heaps in their camps, seemed to form no small portion of their food.

Ludwig Leichhardt, 12 September 1845

A Closer Look

Death by nardoo

Nardoo is a common fern that lives in shallow water across inland Australia. Its spore pods are not only poisonous to people, but can also be fatal to other mammals like sheep, cattle, horses, dogs and camels.

Nardoo contains thiaminase, an enzyme that breaks down the thiamine (also called vitamin B1) in your body. This means that when you eat nardoo, your body's thiamine is destroyed. Thiamine is essential for the body to be able to release the energy from food. Eating nardoo leads to the disease beriberi, unless you treat the nardoo first so that the thiaminase is destroyed. The Aboriginal way of preparing nardoo cakes by rinsing the flour and then baking the cakes got rid of the toxic enzyme.

Burke and Wills ate unprepared nardoo. If they had prepared the nardoo as the Aboriginal people did, they might not have died. We know from Wills' diary and from John King, the only survivor of the party, that shortly before dying, Burke suffered badly from the cold, was very weak and had leg and back pain. We also know that Wills' pulse became extremely slow, his legs and arms were very thin, and he was too weak to move. These were all symptoms of beriberi. When King was the only one left, he managed to stay alive by finding and living with the local Aboriginal group, but he suffered permanent nerve damage in both legs.

... I cannot understand this Nardu at all it certainly will not agree with me in any form we are now reduced to it alone and we manage to get from four to five pounds per day between us. the stools it causes are enormous and seem greatly to exceed the quantity of bread consumed and is very slightly altered in appearance from what it was when eaten.

William John Wills, 20 June 1861

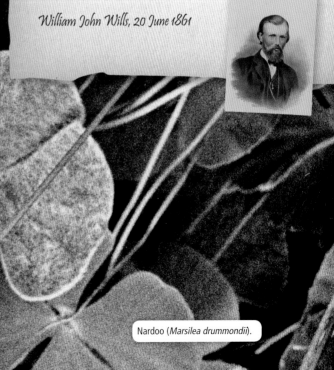

Nardoo (*Marsilea drummondii*).

Hunting

Wills had also traded with friendly Aboriginal people for some fish in April and May 1861. After the Aboriginal people had left, and not being successful at catching his own fish, he once chased some crows off a fish they'd been eating. At another time, it was only luck that presented him with a meal.

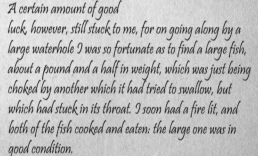

... Having rested a while and eaten a few fish-bones, I moved down the creek, hoping by a late march to be able to reach our own camp; but I soon found, from my extreme weakness, that that would be out of the question. A certain amount of good luck, however, still stuck to me, for on going along by a large waterhole I was so fortunate as to find a large fish, about a pound and a half in weight, which was just being choked by another which it had tried to swallow, but which had stuck in its throat. I soon had a fire lit, and both of the fish cooked and eaten: the large one was in good condition.

William John Wills, 2 June 1861

Mostly, the explorers hunted their meat. In November 1839, John Lort Stokes killed a kangaroo at long range while it was travelling fast. A few days later, he realised that kangaroos which are in a valley always travelled in a curve. They escaped hunters by hopping along the valley before turning slowly up the nearest hill and then going straight up. Stokes would send a man along near the river, while he stayed ahead, well up the hill. As the man by the river startled the kangaroos, they curved up towards Stokes, who shot them at close range.

Admiral John Lort Stokes.

A fanciful illustration of a kangaroo being killed. Stokes claimed that he and a Dr Barker held the kangaroo's tail to stop it clawing the dog with its hind feet. At least one of them should've ended up with a broken leg, as a kangaroo's tail is very solid and can move fast, clubbing anyone standing behind.

Explorers had to eat whatever they could get and, sometimes, they even liked it: Peter Warburton loved camel's foot and enjoyed a cormorant; Phillip Parker King enjoyed eating 'Blue Mountainers', the old name for rainbow lorikeets; John Oxley's party ate a dingo; Stokes ate an 'alligator' (a crocodile, which he said tasted like veal); William Carron killed and ate a dying kangaroo dog; Francis Gregory tried eating a bat but didn't like it; Ernest Giles killed and ate raw a small joey which he found in the desert; John McDouall Stuart ate wallaby, possum, duck, pigeon and kangaroo mice; and Ludwig Leichhardt really enjoyed goanna, possum, wallaby, dried emu and kangaroo meat, stewed cockatoo, crow and eagle—he even consumed the greenhide (unpreserved animal skin) case that held his plant specimens after he was forced to abandon the collection.

A BRIGHT NEW YEAR

Shooting possums by moonlight.

Three Europeans join Aboriginal men on a kangaroo hunt.

Some of the additions to the diet came about when somebody caught a 'new' animal for a scientific collection, and found that it had already been collected. Instead of going into the specimen collection, these animals went into the pot.

Catching an 'alligator'.

Peter Warburton's party. Most of the camels ended up as food.

Preserving meat

When explorers ran out of supplies, were unsuccessful at hunting native animals, or could not rely on local Aboriginal people to supply food, they became desperate and had to kill their packhorses and camels to survive. So that it wouldn't go rotten and be wasted, the meat was smoked and dried. It had all the goodness of fresh meat, but it was lighter to carry and didn't become 'tainted' (the polite way of saying that the meat had gone rotten). After the death of Rajah, their last camel, Burke and Wills cut off his flesh and dried it. This supply of meat ran out after about five weeks.

When food is hung over a smoky fire, it dries out so germs and mould can't grow on it. Salt also stops germs and mould from growing, but makes the meat inedible. Watkin Tench carried salt pork in barrels, but before eating it, he had to soak it in fresh water to get rid of the salt. Tinned food was better, because the food had been boiled to kill all the germs and then sealed in tins to keep germs out. It also had the advantage of being ready to eat.

Tinned meat was invented about the time serious exploring got under way. On Christmas Day, 1813, George Evans was west of the Blue Mountains in New South Wales. It was 'so hott the Fish will not bite,' he wrote, but he had a useful reserve, 'therefore I opened my tin case of Roasted Beef.'

Tinned meat was still a novelty in 1820 when Lieutenant King and his party ate on a hill, which he named 'Donkin's Hill after the inventor of the preserved meats; upon a canister of which our party dined'.

By the 1890s, the novelty of tinned food had worn off. David Carnegie wrote that it was 'good, sometimes excellent; but when you find that a cunning storekeeper has palmed off all his minced mutton on you, you are apt to fancy tinned fare monotonous!' According to Carnegie, it didn't matter what the label said, the tin always contained minced mutton, and so he and his companions were delighted when they could kill an emu. One emu, he said, was all eaten, except for the feathers, bones and beak.

Lieutenant (later Admiral) Phillip Parker King.

Planting seeds

Many early explorers planted seeds as they travelled, possibly to prove that they'd visited the area, or perhaps to provide food for later travellers. Phillip Parker King and Allan Cunningham did a lot of planting when they went ashore during their voyages along the Australian coast in 1818–1821. By 1817, Emperor of the French, Napoleon Bonaparte, had been defeated, and France and Britain were at peace. But the French were interested in establishing a colony or colonies in the western half of Australia, so maybe Cunningham's crops were a way of saying that they (the British) were there first.

Instructions from the British Government in London told him to leave 'some evidence which cannot be mistaken of your having landed', such as a flagpole or a garden. It sounds as if it wanted to show that the British had been there before.

Perhaps planting seeds was just the usual practice, because Cunningham carried out plantings in inland New South Wales, where there was no risk of the French wanting a colony. Long before that, in 1801, King's father, Governor Philip Gidley King, had told James Grant to plant seeds in places where other ships might visit in the following years.

Grant reported later that he had planted wheat, onions, potatoes, cucumber, pumpkin and 'mellon seeds'. He also planted apple seeds, plum and peach stones, and 'a few grains of rice and coffee', as well as setting up the posts for a house, which he hoped might be useful to somebody one day.

Explorers had to use whatever seeds they could get wherever they were and, as they were often on the move, they couldn't water or look after their gardens.

In this project, you will see how many things will grow if they're just poked into the ground and left. What would you plant?

How to do it:

1. With your parents' permission, select a small section of the garden. (Pots will do but the soil in pots dries out more quickly than in the garden.)

2. Choose your seeds and draw a rough plan of what to plant where.

3. Prepare some labels by slitting the drinking straws open along half their length with the scissors. (Be careful or ask an adult to help.) Ask somebody else to hold the straw open while you write the names of the seeds on the inside. When you let the straw go, it will curl around and protect the writing from the sun and rain. If you're by yourself, it's easier to flatten the slit straw and write on the outside.

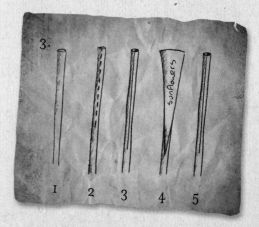

PROJECT   PLANTING SEEDS

4. Plant your seeds a few centimetres down in the ground. Place the straws just behind the seeds to indicate where and what they are, and wait. It might be cheating to water them, but you could make it 'rain' with some help from a watering can!

5. Check the garden once a week to see what has sprouted. Your straw markers will tell you whether the new shoots belong to your seeds or to weeds.

What else you can do:

You could also experiment with one sort of seed (e.g. cherry pips) and plant them at different depths to see what depth is best for them.

Checklist

⊙ seeds e.g. stones of plums, peaches or cherries; seeds of a pumpkin, watermelon or an apple; tomatoes, peas or beans; maybe wheat or corn (some seeds are sterile and won't grow.)

⊙ some plastic drinking straws

⊙ a pair of scissors with thin blades

⊙ a permanent felt-tipped pen with a fine point

⊙ a patch of soil that you can use for a few months

!

Remember that adults get upset when their tools are left out in the rain, or their precious plants are dug up!

Recipe for damper

Making damper is an old bush tradition, and all of the explorers took flour and salt with them to make bread, but the tradition is far older than that—Aboriginal Australians have always cooked damper using flour made from grass seeds, wattle seeds or nardoo.

Try cooking damper at home in an oven or on a camp fire when you go camping.

Oven-cooked damper

Ingredients
2 cups self-raising flour
½ teaspoon salt
1 ½ cups milk
1 teaspoon sugar
1 teaspoon butter

Method

Sift the flour, sugar and salt into a bowl. Then add the butter and enough milk to make a firm dough. Shape into a flat ball and place on a greased and floured oven tray. Bake at 220°C for 25–30 minutes, brushing it with milk as it cooks.

Traditional damper

Traditional bush damper is made out of just flour, salt and water. Use the same amount of flour as for oven-cooked damper, a pinch of salt and just enough water to make a stiff dough. If the dough gets too sloppy, add a bit more flour.

Cook the dough by burying it in the coals of a fire, and brushing off the ash and charcoal before you eat it. You could also experiment with aluminium foil, then publish your method on the Internet and become famous!

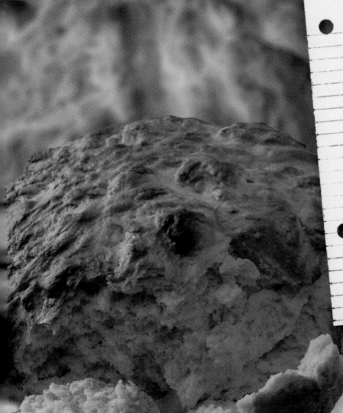

Recipe for steamed newspaper fish

This is a handy survival trick if you happen to have a newspaper with you. If you haven't got newspaper, banana leaves will work.

Steamed newspaper fish

Ingredients and equipment
medium-sized fish
kitchen knife
2 or 3 sheets of a large newspaper
water
maybe a few slices of lemon and onion
coals of a fire, or a barbecue that can be turned low
barbecue tongs

Method

First, catch your fish (or buy it). Slit the belly very carefully (get an adult to help) and remove the guts if you wish. If you leave them in, it doesn't matter, because they just shrivel. There's no need to scale the fish.

Poke in a few slices of lemon and onion, then lay the fish on a sheet of newspaper and wrap it securely. Pour water over the parcel and make it sopping wet. Now wrap it in a second sheet of paper and wet that as well. (The wet newspaper shouldn't catch fire, but always be prepared for bad things. Get an adult to help.)

Two sheets are enough to cook a fish, seven minutes a side. Lay the parcel on the coals of a fire or on a low barbecue (an open grill, not a plate) for seven minutes, lift it off and turn it over to cook for another seven minutes. Then take it off with the tongs and unwrap it carefully.

The skin should stick to the paper and peel off, leaving you with the steamed meat, which you can lift off onto a plate. Then turn the fish over with the tongs and lift the meat from the other side.

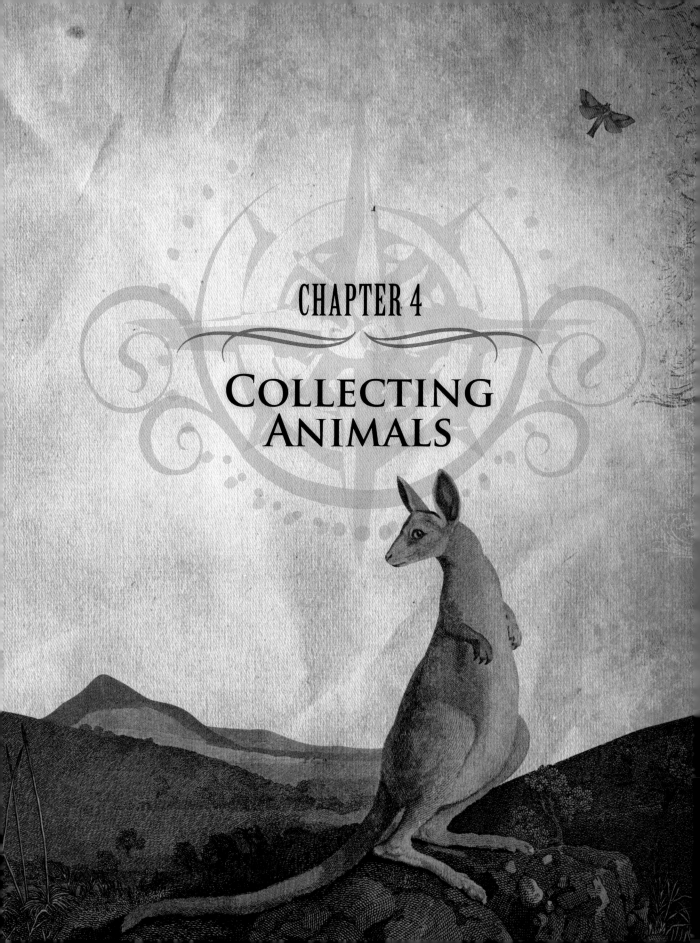

CHAPTER 4

COLLECTING ANIMALS

Birds and other animals

In the eighteenth and nineteenth centuries, scientists were part of expeditions. Natural history (the study of animals and plants) was very fashionable at the time and scientists rushed to be the first to collect and describe plant and animal specimens that Europeans had never seen before. They shot birds and animals and sent their skins and body parts, such as skulls, skeletons and teeth, back to Europe. Sometimes whole dead animals were shipped back, preserved in casks of spirits (alcohol), to stop them from decomposing. There's a story about a servant in England who, in 1799, was carrying a cask containing the bodies of a platypus and a wombat on her head when the bottom of the cask broke and she was covered with foul-smelling liquid. This was bad enough but it was the sight of the bodies of the strangest animals she'd ever seen that really horrified her.

But it wasn't just scientists who were excited by these discoveries. People in Europe were fascinated by the new animals from the other side of the world. Animal skins went to specialists, called taxidermists, who would stuff and sew the skins back into something that matched the sketches and descriptions. Visiting museums, where stuffed specimens were

This king-parrot, painted by Sarah Stone in 1790 in England, has been placed on a branch of a European tree because the artist didn't know what Australian trees looked like.

In the nineteenth century, glass domes like this one containing Australian native birds were popular ornaments in people's homes.

on display, was a popular pastime, and well-off people even bought stuffed birds and animals as ornaments for their homes. People also visited zoos to see some of the few colourful parrots and unusual mammals that had survived the three-month sea journey from Australia.

Artists in Europe also used sketches, descriptions and skins to create illustrations of the new animals, which often they'd never seen alive. This was why the animals in their paintings sometimes looked odd. The colours of Sarah Stone's king-parrot, for example, are faded, its feathers are ruffled and its body looks too long and thin, maybe because she had used an under-stuffed king-parrot as a model.

Finding gold and silver was more popular than collecting unusual animals and plants but, if an explorer couldn't come back with news of rich mineral deposits or land suitable for agriculture, then skins, bones and sketches of strange animals, and pressed flowers and the seeds of new plants were a good alternative.

Joseph Banks joined Captain James Cook's voyage around the world on the *Endeavour*. Although he was mainly a botanist, Banks and his collectors never missed a chance to sample the animals as well. On 14 July 1770, on the east coast of New Holland (Australia), he got his first close look at a kangaroo that had been shot. The following day, he joined others from the *Endeavour* in having kangaroo meat for dinner.

In August, Banks noted that the name that Aboriginal people gave the mysterious animal was 'kangooroo' and James Cook also mentioned its name in his journal.

To compare it to any European animal would be impossible as it has not the least resemblance of any one I have seen. Its fore-legs are extremely short, and of no use to it in walking; its hind again as disproportionately long; with these it hops seven or eight feet at a time.

Joseph Banks, 14 July 1770

Besides the Animals which I have before mentioned, called by the Natives Kangooroo, or Kanguru, here are Wolves, Possums, an Animal like a ratt, and snakes, both of the Venemous and other sorts. Tame Animals here are none except Dogs, and of these we never saw but one, who frequently came about our Tents to pick up bones, etc.

James Cook, 4 August 1770

Europeans found it a challenge to draw animals that they'd never seen alive and that didn't come close to anything they had experienced before. This 1773 image by British painter George Stubbs was the first printed picture of a kangaroo that people in the Northern Hemisphere saw. He based his picture on the skin of a kangaroo that had been shot and collected at the Endeavour River in 1770, taken back to England and stuffed—badly.

The early illustrations of kangaroos were often unrealistic. This picture of a 'kangooroo' was only the second printed image of a kangaroo. It didn't appear until 16 years after Stubbs' image. The picture of a kangaroo (made about 1840) on page 36 was still not right, but it was better than this.

THE KANGOOROO.

This 1807 picture of a wombat family shows that the species wasn't understood then. Wombats have only one baby and don't live in pairs, the male and female coming together only to mate.

The first live kangaroo was sent to England in 1790 and was put on display in London. There were queues of people who each paid a shilling to view 'the wonderful Kanguroo from Botany Bay'.

Platypuses, wombats and koalas weren't noticed by Europeans for around another ten years, probably because they weren't out and about in the daytime. In 1803, Banks sent Robert Brown on a collecting trip in New South Wales and Tasmania. Brown complained in a letter to Banks that he'd seen no new mammals, though there were lots of new fish still to be collected and he had a few new birds to send. He changed his tune in September when he reported 'a new and remarkable species of *Didelphis*' (by which he meant a kind of possum). It came from south of Botany Bay, he said, adding that it was 'called by the natives coloo or coola, and most nearly approaches to the wombat'. Brown was talking about a koala. It must've still been alive because he said his description wasn't perfect, as 'the animal will not submit to be closely inspected, and I have not had the opportunity of dissecting one'.

This picture of a koala was published in the 1880s.

A mounted koala and baby on display in the 1890s.

A Closer Look

Taxidermy

When you last went to a museum, you probably saw dead animals on display. Taxidermy is the art of preserving animal skins to create lifelike animals for display, and someone who does this is called a taxidermist. The word is from the Greek words *taxis*, which means arrangement, and *derma*, which means skin.

Taxidermy became popular in the first half of the nineteenth century when natural history was an exciting new field. Professional and amateur scientists travelled all over the world to collect exotic animals. Their skins were sewn up and stuffed with wood shavings, straw and other material until it looked something like the living animal and then sold to collectors, museums and universities, and also to individuals who just wanted them as curiosities. The animals that were prepared like this were called 'stuffed' animals. The popularity of natural history meant that great numbers of wild animals were slaughtered, many ending up being stuffed. In those days, nobody worried about extinction. Of course, now there are laws that protect many species.

Later in the nineteenth century, the stuffing technique had to change because museums wanted to display specimens that looked much more lifelike. The new techniques, which remain much the same today, included skinning the animal and cutting the head off from the base of the skull. An exact replica of the animal's body was made by either carving balsa wood or by using fine wood shavings or other fibres. Wire was used for the neck, the tail and the legs. The brain was scooped out of the skull with a small spoon. The skin was then carefully placed around the artificial body and sewn up. Specimens prepared in this way are called 'mounted' specimens.

Mounted wallabies posed in lifelike displays in the 1890s.

Bird skins stored in drawers at Museum Victoria.

DiD YOU KNOW ?

How would you describe a platypus to someone who has never seen one before? When the first platypus specimen arrived in Britain from Australia in 1799, scientists couldn't believe their eyes. In fact, they thought it was a fraud and that someone was playing a trick on them by sewing pieces of other animals together. Just imagine what they saw—an animal that had a bill like a duck's, a tail like a beaver's and feet like an otter's. To add to its peculiarities, scientists later discovered that the platypus also laid eggs! No other mammal, except the echidna, lays eggs. (An egg-laying mammal is called a monotreme.)

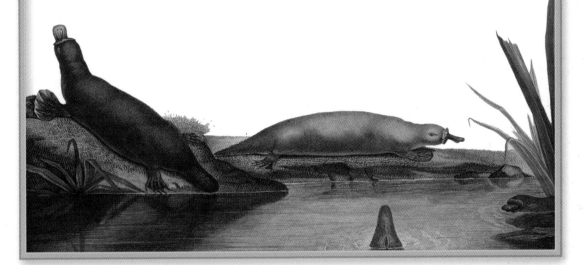

Some strange illustrations of parts of a crocodile, after it'd been killed, from a sketch by Lieutenant Gore of the *Beagle*, 1830s–1840s.

An 'alligator' on the mud, Victoria River, during the Augustus Gregory expedition, 1856. Sometimes, the animals wanted to do the collecting!

Insects and other small creatures

Most people preferred large animals, and it seems that smaller animals just didn't attract the collectors' attention. In his August 1803 letter, Brown wrote that 'insects and shells are neither numerous nor interesting'. Of course, Brown was wrong—Australia's cicadas, moths, beetles, stick insects and other small creatures are all amazing.

Back in 1803, spiders and scorpions were often referred to as 'insects'. A number of the explorers collected spiders, but they weren't often mentioned in their journals, except when Sahleh the camel driver was bitten by a scorpion on the hand as he slept by the fire. It happened on Peter Warburton's 1873 expedition at the time when the members of the party were very weak from hunger and exhaustion. Scorpions are attracted by the light of a fire but, at a certain point, the heat stops them going closer, and they begin to circle the campfire. Sahleh was probably blocking the scorpion's circling. By the next day, he had lost the use of both the bitten hand and the arm. Warburton worried that Sahleh might be too weak to recover. On 29 December, Warburton wrote ominously that he thought 'some one—not I—will have to chop his finger off with a tomahawk, or he will lose his arm and his life' but, a few hours later, a rescue party arrived. The men's spirits were raised, but Warburton noted on New Year's Day that Sahleh 'may escape the tomahawk, but can hardly be spared the knife'. After that, Sahleh wasn't mentioned, except for a comment in May that Sahleh had 'left his finger in Roebourne'.

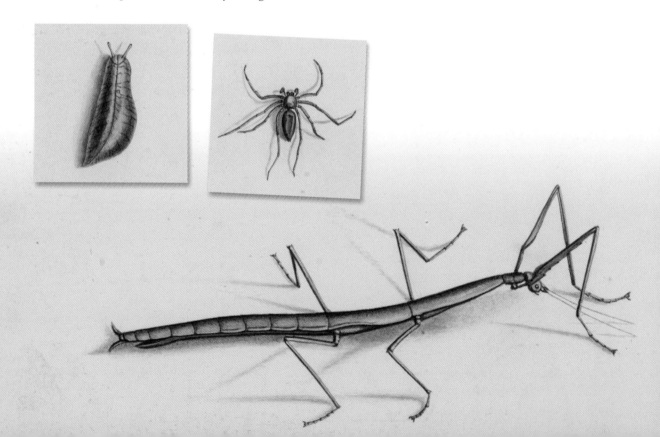

PROJECT

USING AN ARTIST'S BRUSH TO HANDLE SMALL ANIMALS

How to do it:

Find an insect in the garden and put a dry artist's brush near it for it to climb onto. Be careful not to hurt the insect. Leave it on the brush or move it into a container to examine. After you've finished looking at the insect, return it to where you found it.

You can also pick up small water insects, spiders or shrimps using the same method.

Checklist

- *a soft artist's brush (a camel-hair brush between size 3 and size 8 is the best)*

My own favourite brush for this activity is a size 8 that was chewed by silverfish, so it was no good for painting, but it has been moving small animals for 25 years.

PROJECT   FINDING HIDDEN ANIMALS

Using an umbrella is one of the best ways to discover the insects that live on a branch or bush. This project shows you why and how.

How to do it:

Open the umbrella, turn it upside down, hold it under a leafy branch and give the branch a good shake. All sorts of insects will fall into your umbrella. After you stop shaking the branch, watch for 15–20 seconds because some of the insects will hide for a short time by staying still on the umbrella.

Checklist

an umbrella—you can get good results with a black or a white one. A black and white umbrella is even better because light-coloured animals show up against the black cloth and dark ones show up against the white.

When you get excited about your good catch, just remember to keep the umbrella spokes away from people's eyes.

PROJECT   MAKING A POOTER

A pooter is a neat device that uses suction to pick up small animals safely. It's better than a small brush because the animals are held in a container that's easy to empty into another container.

How to do it:

1. Cut the tubing into a 40-centimetre and a 20-centimetre piece.

2. Remove the lid of the bottle and, with adult help, drill two holes, side by side and fit the tubes.

3. With the lid off, wrap and tape two layers of the cloth around the long tube, then pull it back up, so that the filter is near the underside of the lid. Leave the short tube so that it almost reaches the bottom of the bottle. Put the lid back on.

4. Use the glue or sticky tape to hold the tubes in place. You can even use candle wax, but get an adult to help you. If you choose the size of the drill bit carefully, you can probably do without the glue.

5. Find a small insect and put the short tube over it and suck on the long tube to draw it into the pooter. When you have finished looking at the insect, take it back to where you found it and let it go.

Checklist
- a small clear plastic bottle
- 60 cm of plastic tubing (3–4 mm wide)
- a drill and a drill bit slightly smaller than the tubing
- a small piece of fine cloth
- some sticky tape, or some epoxy glue (like Araldite) for a permanent pooter
- scissors

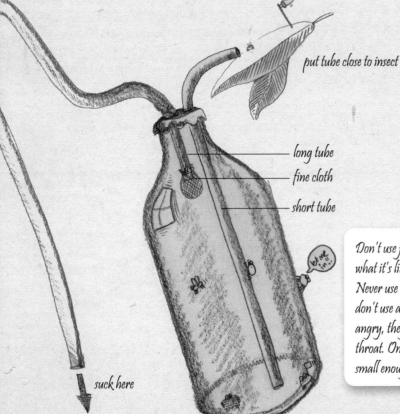

put tube close to insect

long tube
fine cloth
short tube

suck here

Don't use just a tube as a pooter, or you'll soon find out what it's like to have a beetle or a fly caught in your throat. Never use a pooter unless the cloth filter is in place! And don't use a pooter to collect ants because, when they're angry, they release formic acid, which will give you a sore throat. One more thing—only use a pooter on animals small enough to fit into the tube without being hurt.

PROJECT — MAKING AN INSECT LIGHT TRAP

Have you ever noticed how insects fly to a light at night? In this project, you're going to attract them to an illuminated sheet, not to the light itself.

How to do it:

This project needs adult supervision as there is a small chance of getting burnt or of the sheet catching fire if the light touches it. And, having an electric light outside on an extension cord is always a bit risky.

1. Hang the sheet on a wall, a clothesline or a stretched rope. Place the lamp at the base of the sheet so that the light is shining on the sheet but so that it can't touch it.

2. Now all you need to do is wait for the insects to land on the sheet. Either catch the insects with a pooter (see page 55) if they are small, or just look at them (you could use a magnifying glass) until they fly away.

Checklist

- a bright light such as an electric desk lamp, a gas camp light or a very bright torch
- an old sheet (white is best) and somewhere to hang it
- a still night, preferably just after rain

!

Don't put the light too close to the sheet—it could catch fire. And don't leave the lamp unattended, especially on a windy night because the sheet might blow onto the lamp. You catch more insects on a still night anyhow.

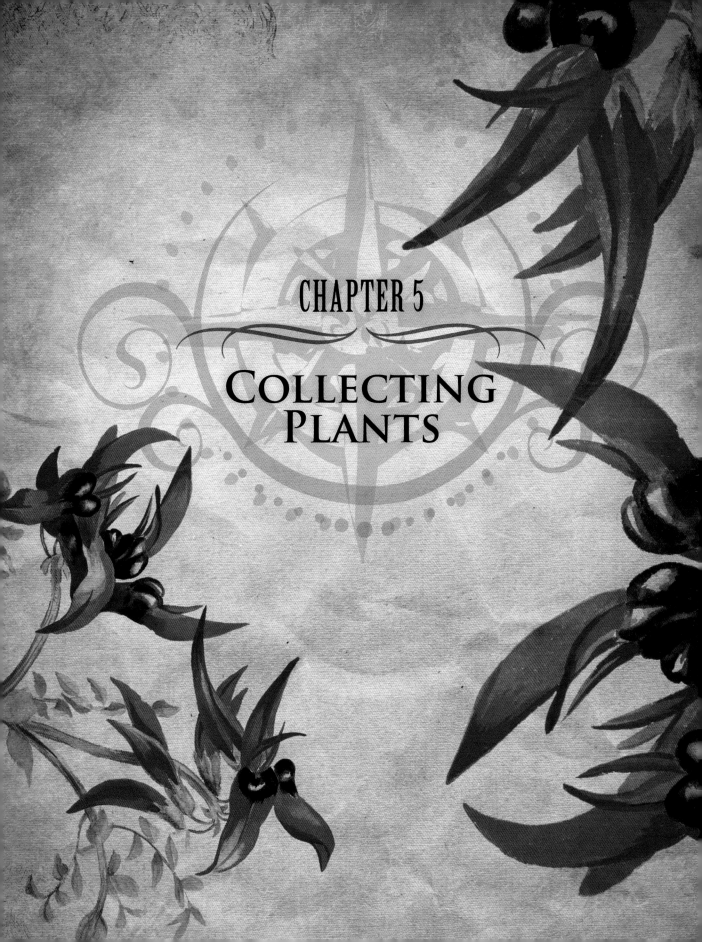

CHAPTER 5

COLLECTING PLANTS

The search for valuable plants

Sir Joseph Banks was annoyed in 1798 that Australian explorers had failed to reach the inland and find any suitable raw materials. Banks saw exploration as having one goal, and that was profit for England. He couldn't believe that Australia, 'in a most fruitful climate, should not produce some native raw material of importance to a manufacturing country as England is'.

Like collecting animals, collecting plants was a fashionable science, but even the men of science wanted to find valuable plants. They hoped to grow rich from new fibres like cotton, new timbers like sandalwood and teak, new food crops like the potato and breadfruit, and even plant materials that could be used in medicines or to dye cloth.

Timber was a high priority. Allan Cunningham examined the cypress pines of the western plains of New South Wales. He'd been told they might make excellent booms and spars for sailing ships, but he found that the wood had too many knots in it, which would make it brittle. Besides that, in those days timber was transported by floating it on the sea or down rivers, and the cypress pines were too far from the sea or any river. So the search continued.

Cunningham was sent out with Lieutenant Phillip Parker King in 1817 on the *Mermaid* to sail along the coast and seek valuable plants there. King was told to look for useful vegetables and any woods suitable for ship-building, cabinet work and household furniture. He was also asked to collect small plant specimens, to number and record them, and to pay special attention to how easily logs of various species would float down rivers to the sea, where they could be loaded on ships.

Allan Cunningham collected specimens at Careening Bay while the *Mermaid* was being repaired in 1817.

This plant specimen was collected in 1998 and is kept at the Australian National Herbarium in Canberra. The specimen label includes a lot of information—the plant's scientific names, who collected it, exactly where and when, a description (such as the colour of the flower) and the kind of country and soils it was growing in.

Flora of AUSTRALIA
AUSTRALIAN NATIONAL HERBARIUM (CANB)

SCROPHULARIACEAE

Derwentia derwentiana (Andrews) B.G.Briggs & Ehrend.
subsp. *derwentiana*

det. B.J. Lepschi 1998

AUSTRALIA: New South Wales

0.4 km E of Coryah Gap Trail on main Mt Kaputar - Narrabri
Road, c. 3.5 km WSW of summit of Mt Kaputar.

30° 17' 04" S   150° 08' 15" E

Rocky, pale-beige loam on road cutting / steep slope. Tall
Eucalyptus spp. forest with understorey of saplings and shrubs.

Corolla pale mauve-white.

Fairly common.

B.J. Lepschi 4104
& J.R. Connors   12 Dec 1998

Dups: (6) B, CDA, L, MO, P, US

CANB 621770.1

Keeping records

It's easy to gather bits of plant and press them for art and craft projects, but scientists have to make much more of an effort with their plant specimens. They have to keep accurate records of where the plants came from, and preserve samples of each new species. Explorers dried and pressed plants, trying to include their leaves, flowers and fruits, which were all useful in identification of the species. Along with these samples, they also gathered seeds to send back to the Royal Botanic Gardens, Kew, just outside London.

You might think that plant collecting would be a harmless occupation, but there are hidden dangers. John Murphy, a boy in Ludwig Leichhardt's party, found this out the hard way, after he put some seeds inside his shirt, causing his skin to blister.

This specimen (*Eucalyptus platyphylla*) was one of many that botanists Joseph Banks and Daniel Solander collected at Endeavour River, Queensland, while the *Endeavour* was being repaired in July 1770.

John Murphy, having no pockets in his trowsers, put the seeds which he found during the stage into his bosom, close to the skin, where he had already deposited a great number of Sterculia, and was much inconvenienced by the starry prickles which surround the seeds. Afterwards, finding the drooping Grevillea in fruit, he gathered some capsules and placed them as before stated. Upon arriving at the camp, he felt great pain; and, on examining the place, he saw, to his greatest horror, that the whole of the skin of the epigastric region was coloured black, and raised into a great number of painful blisters. Upon his showing it to me, I thought that it was caused by the Sterculia prickles having irritated the skin, and rendered it more sensitive to the sharp properties of the exudation of the seed-vessels of Grevillea. Brown, however, merely touched the skin of his arm with the matter, when blisters immediately rose; showing clearly its properties. The discoloration of the skin was like the effects of nitrate of silver.

Ludwig Leichhardt, 22 September 1845

The fate of specimens

Many of the explorers' plant specimens found their way to the Royal Botanic Gardens, Kew, where they remain to this day. There, they are kept in a herbarium, a building that's full of collections of preserved specimens. But there were plant specimens that never made it to England. Leichhardt said he wept when he had to abandon both his collection of plant specimens and those of John Gilbert.

William Carron, the botanist on the Kennedy expedition on Cape York, had to be rescued from angry Aborigines, and fled with a parcel containing the seeds of 87 species, but he had to leave his collection of specimens behind.

Animal pests were always a problem for plant specimens on ships, and Lieutenant King once had his cutter, the *Mermaid*, submerged in Sydney Harbour, hoping to drown all the rats and cockroaches on board but, before long, the cockroaches were back again. Mice, rats and cockroaches all made holes in food containers and spoiled the food, but they also threatened scientific specimens on a number of ships.

Joseph Banks managed to save his specimens when the *Endeavour* struck a reef in 1770, but Robert Brown complained to Banks in 1803 that his own specimens were at risk. One ship was too damp for the dried specimens. On another ship, the specimens had been carried to Sydney 'between the beams of the bread-room, where, altho' they remained tolerably dry, yet they suffered very much from mice and insects'.

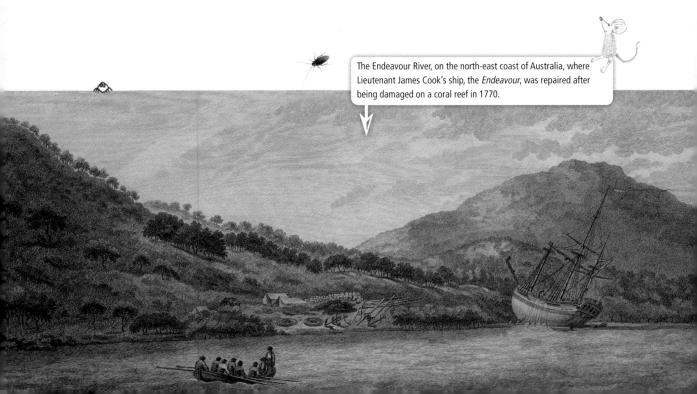

The Endeavour River, on the north-east coast of Australia, where Lieutenant James Cook's ship, the *Endeavour*, was repaired after being damaged on a coral reef in 1770.

Sturt's desert pea, named after Charles Sturt.

A Closer Look

Carl Linnaeus' scientific naming system

Have you ever wondered how plants get their names? It's not all accidental: there's a scientific system in place controlling how it all happens. Around 250 years ago, a Swedish scientist named Carl Linnaeus invented a system for naming all living things using a two-word Latin description. Examples of his naming system are *Homo sapien*s to describe a human being and *Tyrannosaurus rex* for a particular kind of dinosaur. By the time botanists were naming Australia's unusual plants and animals, the Linnaean system was being used worldwide and was adopted here too.

According to Linnaeus' system, the first word in a plant's name describes the genus (the general name of the group of plants) and the second word describes the species (the specific name for a particular plant in that group).

The scientific names of some Australian plants are named after the people who found them, such as botanists Allan Cunningham and Joseph Banks and explorer Edmund Kennedy: *Bauhinia cunninghamii*, *Banksia ericifolia* and *Kennedia rubicunda* are just a few. Other names tell us what the plant looks like, such as the colour of the flowers or the shape of the leaves (e.g. *longifolia* means long leaves and *alba* means white). And others celebrate the place where the plant grows (e.g. the cycad found on rocky ranges and gorges in the MacDonnell Ranges is called *Macrozamia macdonnelli*).

Can you guess why the plants in this list have these names?

Hibiscus grandiflora
Eucalpytus odorata
Pimelea rosea
Limonium baudinii
Nauclea leichhardti
Dendrobium stuartii

Eremophila longifolia

Correa alba

DID YOU KNOW ?

Nineteenth-century explorers didn't come near to collecting all the plant species in Australia. In 2007, in Western Australia, for example, there were over 1500 plant specimens collected but not yet described or named by scientists.

Species, new to scientists, are being noticed because there are areas of land that companies want to clear, such as for building houses and for mining. But the land has to be surveyed first before the government agrees to the use of the land or not.

New species are still appearing, but we are losing other species through extinction. Since European settlement in Australia in 1788, around 60 plant species have become extinct and 1240 are in danger of becoming extinct.

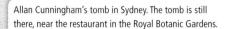

Allan Cunningham's tomb in Sydney. The tomb is still there, near the restaurant in the Royal Botanic Gardens.

Banksia ericifolia, named after botanist Joseph Banks.

PROJECT

MAKING A SIMPLE PLANT PRESS

Pressed and dried plants can keep for hundreds of years—specimens collected by Joseph Banks and Daniel Solander in 1770 are available today for professional botanists to study. The trick is to squash the specimens flat between sheets of paper while they dry. Banks dried his specimens in the sun, but a plant press is better and the newspaper can be recycled after you've finished.

How to do it:

1. Collect some plant specimens but be careful in case they have prickles or spines, or cause allergic reactions.

2. Put each specimen inside a folded newspaper sheet.

3. Place a few sheets of newspaper on one piece of cardboard, followed by a specimen (in its folded sheet of newspaper). Add a few more newspaper sheets and then another specimen, and so on. When you've finished stacking the sheets in this way, place the other piece of cardboard on top.

4. Tie the plant press up tightly with rope or use bricks to apply pressure. Each day, replace the newspaper sheets, even the ones containing the specimens, with dry newspaper.

Checklist

- plenty of sheets of newspaper
- two sheets of thick flat cardboard, larger than the newspaper
- plant specimens
- some string, rope or straps to tie the plant press together, or maybe several bricks to sit on top of the plant press

!

Pressing flowers in a book may be fun, but it usually stains the pages, which might not please your parents!

What else you can do:

1. Glue some dried flowers onto a rectangle of coloured cardboard and cover it with clear contact paper to make a bookmark.

2. Create an artwork by arranging a delicate plant, such as a creeper, on paper to make an interesting pattern. Glue it in place and then experiment further using paint or any other techniques to create art.

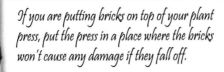

!

If you are putting bricks on top of your plant press, put the press in a place where the bricks won't cause any damage if they fall off.

PROJECT   COLLECTING PLANT SPECIMENS

Many of the explorers not only collected plant specimens, but also had artists in their expeditions to record these plants by drawing or painting them. These days, you can record plants using a camera.

In this project, you will collect plant specimens.

How to do it:

1. Use the secateurs to cut plant specimens. Practise on a few simple plants in your garden first. Take care when you are using the secateurs, or get an adult to help you. If you can, cut a small branch that has flowers and seeds as well as leaves on it. Put each specimen in a plastic bag. The branch should be no more than 33 centimetres long, so that it will fit inside the plant press. If you plan to mount the specimens on A4 paper, reduce this to 25 centimetres.

2. When you collect a plant, you need to record on a slip of paper as many details as you can: collector's name, date, the location where it was collected, the type of soil (sandy soil, clay etc.) and its 'habit' (tree, shrub, creeper, herb etc.). If you can borrow a GPS (Global Positioning System) unit, you can fix the location of the plant accurately. All information is useful, so if you know the main rock types and the difference between heath, dry and wet sclerophyll and rainforest, write that on the collection slip as well. Put the collection slip inside the plastic bag.

3. If you have a camera, take a picture that you can later include with the specimen.

4. After you've collected your specimens, take them out of the plastic bags. Put each one in the middle of a double sheet of newspaper and fold the sheet over. Include its information slip.

5. Stack the specimens (all inside their newspaper sheets) and then put them between the two cardboard sheets of the press, and tie or strap them together. Change the paper daily, making sure that the collection slips stay with the specimens.

6. After a week or so, when the specimens are dry, glue them to the sheets of white paper, along with the collection slips in the bottom right corner.

Remember that some plants are dangerous, as John Murphy learned (see page 59)! Also, many species are now protected and so you aren't allowed to collect them. You can see a list of these species at www.environment.gov.au/cgi-bin/sprat/public/publicthreatenedlist.pl/?wanted=flora

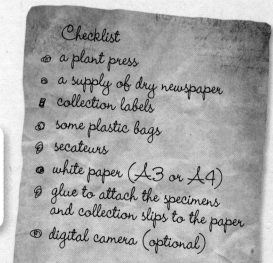

Checklist
- a plant press
- a supply of dry newspaper
- collection labels
- some plastic bags
- secateurs
- white paper (A3 or A4)
- glue to attach the specimens and collection slips to the paper
- digital camera (optional)

CHAPTER 6

JOURNALS AND NOTEBOOKS

The importance of records

One of the main reasons we know so much about explorers' expeditions is because of all the details they recorded in their journals and notebooks. To the people who provided explorers with funds, food and equipment, these records and journals were important. This was especially true if they noted the whereabouts of minerals, good agricultural land and other resources that might be valuable. Details about discoveries were treated with great secrecy so that nobody else would benefit from them. On 5 March 1801, in Sydney, Governor King told Lieutenant James Grant that when Grant and his crew returned to Sydney in the *Lady Nelson*, he must collect together sketches, journals, notes, plans and charts from the ships' crew, seal them up and deliver them straight to him, the governor.

Journals provided the scientific details that might be used to draw maps and charts of the land, the coast and the oceans, as well as descriptions and sketches of plants and animals that Europeans had never seen before. Later, in the published journals, each writer also showed others how to follow their tracks to a particular point, and let them know what they might expect when they got there, including where to find water and food. John Murray, who commanded the *Lady Nelson* after James Grant, was careful to let those who visited later know about good water and food resources after he visited Victoria's Port Phillip in March 1802. John McDouall Stuart also wrote about how he made sure others could find water.

Lieutenant James Cook's journal of his voyage on the *Endeavour*.

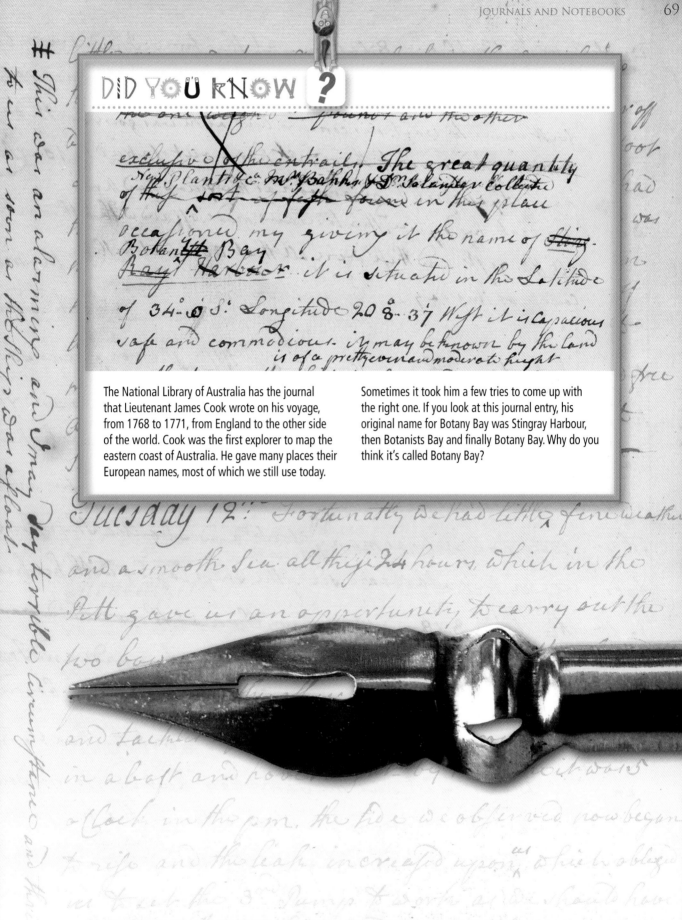

DID YOU KNOW ?

The National Library of Australia has the journal that Lieutenant James Cook wrote on his voyage, from 1768 to 1771, from England to the other side of the world. Cook was the first explorer to map the eastern coast of Australia. He gave many places their European names, most of which we still use today.

Sometimes it took him a few tries to come up with the right one. If you look at this journal entry, his original name for Botany Bay was Stingray Harbour, then Botanists Bay and finally Botany Bay. Why do you think it's called Botany Bay?

A Closer Look

Different versions of an event

Sometimes more than one person kept a journal on an expedition, enabling us to see different versions of the same event. On the voyage of the *Endeavour*, Lieutenant James Cook, botanist Joseph Banks and artist Sydney Parkinson all kept journals.

Here is some of what Cook and Banks wrote on the day that the *Endeavour* struck a reef in north-east Australia and became stranded there for around 24 hours. In those times, spelling and punctuation didn't follow the rules of today.

You can see Cook's handwriting on the background image.

Cook's journal, 11 June 1770

… we went to work to lighten her as fast as possible which seem'd to be the only means we had left to get her off as we went a Shore about the top of High-water - we not only started water but threw'd over board our guns Iron and stone ballast, Casks, Hoops staves oyle Jars, decay'd stores etc many of these last articles lay in the way at coming at heavyer - all this time the Ship made little or no water. At a 11 oClock in the AM being high-water as we thought we try'd to heave her off without success she not being a float by a foot or more notwithstanding by this time we had thrown over board 40 or 50 Tun weight, as this was not found sufficient we continued to Lighten her by every method we could think off As the Tide fell the ship began to make water as much as two Pumps could free

Banks' journal, 11 June 1770

… Orders were now given for lightning the ship which was began by starting our water and pumping it up; the ballast was then got up and thrown over board, as well as 6 of our guns (all that we had upon deck). All this time the Seamen workd with surprizing chearfullness and alacrity; no grumbling or growling was to be heard throughout the ship, no not even an oath (tho the ship in general was as well furnishd with them as most in his majesties service).

H.M. Bark *Endeavour*

Stories of disasters (including deaths of both men and their animals) and achievements, as well as amusing incidents, filled the pages of journals, which many of the writers hoped would be published one day and make them famous (even if they had died during the expedition). Some spoke of their opinions and treatment of members of their teams, others spoke of the conflict and friendship among men, both within the party and with the Aboriginal people of the region.

But, not all journals were valuable and, sometimes, they were just about useless. Governor King explained in a letter to Sir Joseph Banks that he couldn't understand what Francis Barrallier, who'd been sent out to find a way over the Blue Mountains, had written in his journals, as his handwriting was so bad.

The survival of journals

Today, we can make copies of documents and photos on computers but, in the days of the explorers, there was only one copy of their journals and so, if journals were lost, they could never be replaced. For this reason, explorers were determined that, no matter what, their journals had to survive their expeditions. They'd spent a lot of time on their writing and wanted others to be able to read it.

On 7 July 1841, as Edward John Eyre and Wylie came close to Albany in Western Australia, they turned the remaining horses loose and abandoned most of their possessions. But Eyre described how he 'took my journals and charts, and with Wylie forded the river about breast high'. He didn't say so, but the maps and journals would've been wrapped in waterproof oilskins.

At one mile, saw Finniss Springs a mile and a half to the south of us; went down to them and camped. There is an immense quantity of water flowing from them. I shall raise a large cone of stones upon the hill, which is very prominent and can be seen from a long distance.

John McDouall Stuart, 21 April 1859

As far as we are judges, it is ... most excellent water as clear as crystal—lies from the beach about 10 or a dozen yards and plenty of it to water the Grand Fleet of England; it is nearer the entrance than the foot of Arthur's Seat by about 2 miles, and can easily be found out by the land which for a few miles before you come to it is low ... there is plenty of duck about it, but so shy that only two have been shot, a circumstance we did not a little regret as they exceed in flavour any I ever eat.

John Murray, 5 March 1802

Even Burke and Wills understood how important their journals were and, in his field notebook, Wills wrote how, after he, King and Burke fell ill, he made his way back to the Dig Tree on 30 May 1861 to leave their journals safely buried for somebody to find later.

It was a terrible thing for an explorer to lose the scientific collections of pressed plants and seeds, and preserved animals and animal skins. But it was much worse to lose notes, charts, drawings and other records. William Carron, the botanist on Edmund Kennedy's disastrous expedition which ended in Kennedy's death, was forced to abandon the journal of his botanical work.

A page from Wills' diary.

Reached the Depot this morning at 11 oclock, no traces of any one except blacks having been here since we left. Deposited some journals and a notice of our present condition. Started back in the afternoon & camped at the first waterhole.

William John Wills, 30 May 1861

All my specimens were left behind, which I regretted very much: for, though much injured, they contained specimens of very beautiful trees, shrubs, and Orchideae. I could also only secure an abstract of my journal, except that portion of it from 13th November to 30th December, which I have in full. My original journal, with a botanical work which had been kindly lent me by a friend in Sydney for the expedition, was left behind.

William Carron, 30 December 1848

Carron and the other survivors of Kennedy's party had to retreat in a hurry because they feared that the local Aboriginal people, who'd been trading food for fish hooks just a few days before, would attack them. In contrast, in October 1875, when Ernest Giles nearly lost pages from his journal due to a sudden strong wind, some visiting Aboriginal people at his camp in Western Australia helped him save his records.

In 1862, John McDouall Stuart was working his way down to Adelaide after finding an overland route to Australia's northern coast. He was ill and feared that he mightn't survive, but he knew that his journals, which would ensure his fame, would make it back with his men.

While we were at dinner to-day a sudden whirlwind sprang up and sent a lot of my loose papers, from where I had been writing, careering so wildly into the air, that I was in great consternation lest I should lose several sheets of my journal, and find my imagination put to the test of inventing a new one. We all ran about after the papers, and so did some of the blacks, and finally they were all recovered.

Ernest Giles, 16 October 1875

This morning I again feel very ill. I am very doubtful of my being able to reach the settled districts. Should anything happen to me, I keep everything ready for the worst. My plan is finished, and my journal brought up every night, so that no doubt whatever can be thrown upon what I have done. All the difficult country is now passed, and what remains is well known to those who have been out with me before; so that there is no danger of the party not finding their way back, should I be taken away.

John McDouall Stuart, 10 September 1862

PROJECT   KEEPING A JOURNAL

Explorers always tried to keep accurate records of their expeditions in their journals. Today, it's not explorers but tourists who keep journals of their trips. When my two children were 10 and 12, we went to Europe for three months. Their teachers asked them to keep a journal. So, each night, before dinner, they recorded where they'd gone that day, what they'd seen, what happened, what they'd eaten, and what words they'd learned in the local language. They also pasted in tickets, pamphlets and postcards that they'd collected and left spaces for the photos they'd taken.

How to do it:

It's a good idea to number the pages and leave the first two sheets blank, so you can add a contents list later. Talk to your parents about contact information for an 'If lost' notice at the front of your journal.

You want the journal to be interesting, even if only you or your family read it. So each day, work through the checklist of topics I've suggested opposite. Add to the list if you like. Sometimes you might miss out some of the topics and sometimes you might write more than suggested.

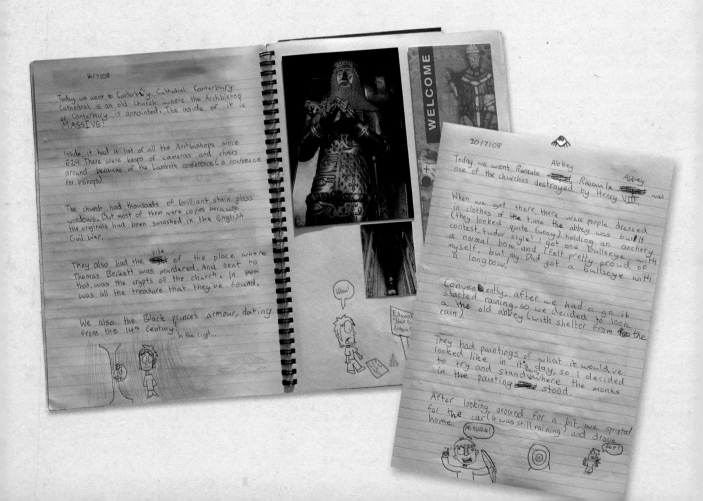

Topics for your journal:

* the date
* where you started your trip
* where you went, how far you went and how long it took
* what you hoped to see and what you actually saw
* the historical background of two things you saw
* two descriptions of interesting places or sights
* details of photos you took
* a map, a sketch or a diagram of a place or places you visited
* two new names, terms, words, facts or ideas
* three funny things
* two surprising facts
* several new animals or plants
* where and what you ate and drank
* what the weather was like
* something you bought
* who you talked to (apart from your family)
* the best thing you saw during the whole day

Checklist

- writing materials: pens, coloured pencils, an eraser, maybe a short ruler
- a book to write in (I've found that the best type of book is a slim 120-page A4 notepad with a spiral binding. This is firm enough for me to sit with it on my lap and write in it.)

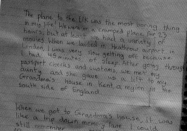

KENT VILLAGES

Don't put anything in your journal that might be embarrassing to somebody else.

Entertaining tales

Journals weren't only for the serious business of science—some explorers wrote parts of their journals to entertain their readers, especially if they thought they would eventually be published. There are tales of narrow escapes with wild animals, floods, fires and attacks by annoyed Aboriginal people defending their land.

There are funny stories as well, like the one Ernest Giles told of a European husband and wife who came to see his camels. Many explorers took small dogs that were easy to feed and would bark at night if there was a disturbance. The ground was too rough for small dogs, so they were usually carried in pouches on the camels. When the couple saw a pup in a bag on each side of the camel, the man asked what they were, and Giles' Aboriginal assistant, Tommy, answered that they were the camel's babies. The man and woman took him seriously, until the man bent down to have a close look at one of the pups, which growled and snapped at his nose. The couple didn't find Tommy's joke funny and they walked away, without saying a word.

Then the tall man said to the wife, 'Oh, lord, look yer, see how they carries their young.' Only the pup's heads appeared, a string round the neck keeping them in; 'but they looks like dogs too, don't they?' With that he put his huge face down, so as to gaze more intently at them, when the little dog, who had been teased a good deal and had got snappish, gave a growl and snapped at his nose.

Ernest Giles, 30 January 1876

Major Mitchell sketching the entrance of the caves in Wellington Valley, New South Wales.

Dogs were often taken on expeditions.

PROJECT DRAWING BIRDS

Explorers made sketches of landscapes, plants and animals in their journals or in their sketchbooks. A couple of hundred years ago, artists didn't mind other artists copying their work. In fact, they were pleased. John Hunter and George Raper, two of the crew on the *Sirius* that sailed to Australia in 1788, spent some of their spare time painting the birds and flowers of New South Wales, and Hunter often copied Raper's work.

How to do it:

1. Look at these two paintings of a pigeon. How are they similar? How are they different?

2. Copy one of the paintings. How does your painting compare to Hunter's and Raper's?

John Hunter's pigeon.

Checklist
- coloured pencils, crayons or paints
- blank paper

George Raper's pigeon.

CHAPTER 7

THE WATER PROBLEM

In nineteenth-century Australia, hygiene standards hardly existed. Most of the water that people used was full of living things, not all of them good. Central Sydney in the 1850s got its water from the swamps near Centennial Park and later from the swamps at Botany Bay, through Busby's Bore. In 1859, a member of the New South Wales Parliament claimed that water from the swamp where City Road meets Parramatta Road, just near the University of Sydney, was being taken by milkmen to top up their milk cans. So the milk was as bad as the water. The swamp is still there, disguised as a lake in Victoria Park.

Other cities were not much better, and so many well-off homes had a dripstone filter, made of a porous sandstone from Norfolk Island, to purify water. Water would be poured into the bowl at the top, and it would slowly filter through to a clean bucket underneath. In January 1859, *Scientific American* published instructions for making a filter to clean rainwater coming from a roof, before it went into a storage tank. This information was then available all around the world.

While city people might've had problems with water, explorers had many more—they needed to find water, they needed good water and they had to carry water. If the only available water was bad, they had to use it anyhow, and that meant they needed to either treat it or put up with it.

January 1859, Scientific American

The way to do this is as follows ▶

Construct a tolerably large and stout wooden box, with a hole in the bottom or at the side near the bottom, and in connection with a pipe leading into the cistern; nail a coarse cotton or linen cloth over its bottom inside, and then fill it up to within three inches of the top with layers of clean gravel, sand, and charcoal, and over the top of these secure a stout cloth. Into this box lead the pipe, and as the rain passes through it to the cistern, it will be purified and fitted for drinking, or any other purpose. The top cloth of this filter can be easily removed and frequently washed. At a little extra cost, this filter may be made so as to rotate on an axis to be turned upside down, and washed out by making clean water rush from its bottom through to the top. It is necessary to make such filters somewhat large to carry off water rapidly during heavy showers.

Instructions for making a filter to purify rainwater in 1859.

A dripstone filter at Cooma Cottage, Yass, the former home of Hamilton Hume.

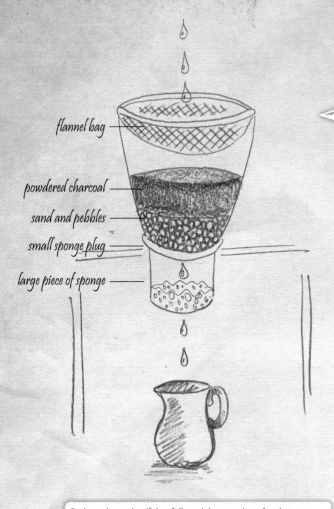

flannel bag

powdered charcoal

sand and pebbles

small sponge plug

large piece of sponge

A copy of a drawing of a water filter from a woman's diary in the 1860s.

Finding water

The explorers learned very early on how to spot signs of fresh water. In 1801, for example, James Grant followed the croaking of frogs to water. Whenever they saw birds, explorers, as a rule, assumed there was water about. John Oxley in 1817, Edward John Eyre in 1840, Ludwig Leichhardt in 1845 and Augustus Gregory in 1846 all followed the screeches of white cockatoos to find water. John McDouall Stuart knew that 'diamond birds' (diamond doves) were in the habit of heading for water in the afternoon and evening, but all the explorers knew that if they followed Aboriginal tracks (either paths or footprints), they would get to water in the end. On top of that, most of them agreed that the smoke of fires indicated that there was water somewhere, because smoke meant Aboriginal people, who wouldn't stay where there wasn't water.

Explorers knew that if they followed the screeches of cockatoos, they'd find water.

John McDouall Stuart knew that diamond doves (the birds on the ground) would lead him to water in the afternoon and evening.

When water was too hard to find, there were last resorts, like the roots of some trees. In 1875, Ernest Giles realised that the local Aboriginal people were also desperate for water when he saw them piercing tree roots to get liquid.

There was worse than tree-root water. Charles Bonney, who was taking cattle overland to Adelaide in 1838, killed a calf to drink its blood. It did little to quench his men's thirst, he said, but 'it restored our strength very much'. The blood would've been cleaner than most of the water, and less salty.

This expedition has found a waterhole. How do you think they found it?

Members of an expedition getting water from a well that they've dug in the sand.

Attempting to use salt water

In many parts of Australia, there are large amounts of salt under the ground. Some salt is formed when rocks break down, but scientists think much of the salt either blew in from the sea as salt spray, over long periods, or that when sea levels were higher than now, large parts of Australia were under the sea. Nobody really knows what the cause is, but the salt is there.

To the explorers, salt water was almost as feared as no water at all. In 1829, Charles Sturt recorded a cry of amazement and 'looks of terror and disappointment' when his men found salt water in the Darling River. Because there was an extreme drought, much of the water entering that part of the river came from salt springs, making the river water undrinkable. And back in those days, Sturt had no way to make fresh water from salt water. His thirsty party had to move on, without a drink.

In 1857, Herschel Babbage went to explore the area near Woomera in South Australia. He took drilling equipment to sink wells, and a still, which is a piece of equipment with a boiler that turns salt water into steam. The steam then cools to make fresh water because the salt is left behind in the boiler. He also took filter paper to remove mud and clay from muddy water. Salt water was rarely muddy but, in the same day, you might be faced with muddy water or salt water, so you had to be ready for both.

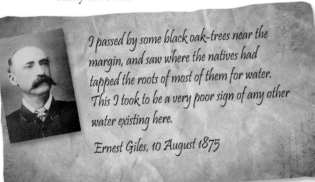

I passed by some black oak-trees near the margin, and saw where the natives had tapped the roots of most of them for water. This I took to be a very poor sign of any other water existing here.

Ernest Giles, 10 August 1875

Drinking foul water

In August 1817, even though Oxley was somewhere between the flooded Lachlan and the Macquarie rivers in New South Wales, he was too far from the rivers and needed to dig for water. His account of trying to make thick muddy water drinkable seems to have set a pattern for later horror tales about water.

Allan Cunningham had described, three months earlier, how his party had boiled and strained the foul water from 'corrupted holes' to destroy the tiny life forms that filled the water. This is very interesting because this was long before anybody officially knew about microbes.

When they wrote up their journals for publication, explorers needed to make them interesting to their readers, and horror tales about water seem to have been popular. Leichhardt described drinking water after straining the mud left after horses and cattle had rolled in it, and Sturt told of 'drinking water' that was so muddy that it stuck to the horses' noses like clay.

But the champion storyteller was Giles, in the 1870s. He wrote of drinking from a 'pool of slime', but that was just the start. One hole, he said, 'was choked up with rotten leaves, dead animals, birds, and all imaginable sorts of filth'. Bubbles were seething out of it, but the tracks and fireplaces around it suggested that Aboriginal people had been drinking from it, so he baled some out for his horse, which managed to force down only one bucketful. The next day, he was still there, but the water level was lower, so he had to use his boot to get water up into the bucket, and he was delighted that the horse didn't want to drink more than one bucketful.

David Carnegie pretended that he could bear awful conditions. He said he drank water so bad that camels refused it, but what he didn't say was that he had a secret way of treating it. He strained the putrid water through a flannel shirt, boiled it, added ashes and Epsom salts (which he believed would improve it, but which probably didn't do anything), and so prepared 'a serviceable beverage'. And these days, people complain about maybe having to drink recycled water!

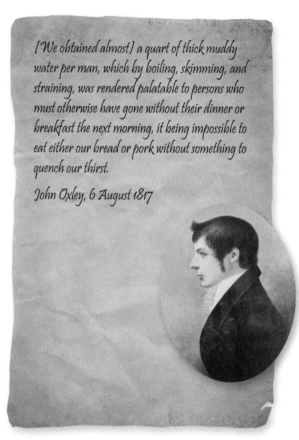

[We obtained almost] a quart of thick muddy water per man, which by boiling, skimming, and straining, was rendered palatable to persons who must otherwise have gone without their dinner or breakfast the next morning, it being impossible to eat either our bread or pork without something to quench our thirst.

John Oxley, 6 August 1817

Most of the explorers would've drunk water like this quite happily.

One of Giles' illustrations from his journal, showing him baling out water from a 'stinking pit' for his horse.

PROJECT   MAKING A WATER FILTER

If the only water you could find was dirty muddy water, you'd need to know how to make a water filter. When you filter water you remove all visible particles from the water, but it might still contain harmful bacteria that the filter can't remove. To make the water safe to drink, you'd also need to use purifying tablets.

How to do it:

1. Cut off the end of the bottle evenly. Be careful or ask an adult for help.

2. Place some cotton wool in the neck of the bottle, as a filter. This will stop the sand from escaping.

3. Turn the bottle upside down and fill it with layers of fine sand, then coarse sand, then fine gravel and finally coarse gravel. The bigger the filter and the more layers you have in it, the better.

4. Pour some muddy water through the filter. Catch it in another container. The water that comes out of the filter should be clear. If it isn't, pour the water through the filter again. The 'clean' water is still likely to contain bacteria. Smell the water but don't drink it!

What else you can do:

1. Find out how long it takes to filter one litre of water.

2. Compare the clearness of the water when you use only a few layers of sand and gravel in your filter and when you use twice as many layers.

large pebbles

small pebbles

coarse sand

sand

fine sand

cotton wool

Checklist

- a large plastic bottle (a 3 or 4-litre juice bottle would work well)
- a waterproof container big enough for the plastic bottle to sit in
- scissors or a sharp knife
- fine and coarse sand
- fine and coarse gravel
- cotton wool

Carrying water—bottles, bags and barrels

In the earliest days, explorers carried their own water in bottles that were protected by a rope or cloth covering, like the one Captain Sturt used. Extra water had to be carried in wooden barrels and, later on, canvas water bags were used. Tradition says that these bags were designed by Major Thomas Mitchell, based on kangaroo-skin water bags that he saw Aboriginal people using.

The water bottle used by Captain Charles Sturt in the 1820s.

The men in John Horrocks' expedition carried water in a barrel when camping in the desert. Horrocks is sitting in a tree because, when the country was flat, this was the only way to see what lay ahead.

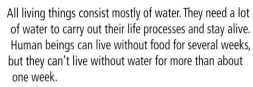

DID YOU KNOW ?

A healthy 12-year-old is about 80% water

A loss of 10% or more of the body's water could mean death

All living things consist mostly of water. They need a lot of water to carry out their life processes and stay alive. Human beings can live without food for several weeks, but they can't live without water for more than about one week.

At birth, 90% of a baby's body is water. In the body of an adult, the water content decreases to 70%, which drops to 50% with age. If you get dehydrated and your body loses 10% or more of its water, you could die.

Have you ever heard that everyone needs to drink eight glasses of water a day? Many people take this advice seriously but scientists are still arguing about how much water a person should drink. People are able to get a lot of water for the day from their food and, when you're healthy, the body also has the ability to maintain its water balance.

The canvas bags would lose a small amount of water to the outside, and when this evaporated, it kept the rest of the water cool. As the canvas got wet, the fibres would swell, reducing the amount of water that could leak through. The canvas bags, like the wooden barrels, were very leaky when they were dry, so they would have to be soaked first, to make the fibres or wood swell.

More than one explorer found himself in trouble when the water containers dried out. To get around this, some expeditions carried metal tanks on carts or in saddlebags on camels. A few people tried using metal tanks with taps fitted, but the taps were often ripped off by rocks or rough bush.

This man is using a canvas water bag.

Sturt and his expedition party had to dig an underground room to shelter from the heat.

The mean of the thermometer for the months of December, January, and February, had been 101 degrees, 104 degrees, and 101 degrees respectively in the shade. Under its effects every screw in our boxes had been drawn, and the horn handles of our instruments, as well as our combs, were split into fine laminae. The lead dropped out of our pencils, our signal rockets were entirely spoiled; our hair, as well as the wool on the sheep, ceased to grow, and our nails had become as brittle as glass.

Charles Sturt, 14 April 1845

The Sturt expedition out of food and water.

A Closer Look

Water in Australia

Australia has always been called a dry continent. Much of it certainly looks dry but, in some parts of Australia, there's still quite a lot of water, deep down, that soaked in many thousands of years ago. However, there's not as much now as there used to be.

The Great Artesian Basin lies beneath 22% of the continent. Most of the water comes from the wet tropics of Queensland, soaking down into porous rocks. It makes an extremely slow journey through the rock, advancing probably between one and five metres a year. If the water's not tapped by a well, it eventually emerges at springs in central Australia.

The route that John McDouall Stuart followed through South Australia went along a line of these springs, which are known as 'mound springs' because the salts in the water form crystal masses that pile up around each opening.

In the past, wells were drilled to get the water and, in many places, any excess water was allowed to flow out into the desert and evaporate. We realise now that a lot of artesian water has been wasted and it could take thousands of years to replace it.

Australia's in a drought again, a long drought, and nobody can say when it'll end, or even if it will. We waste water on gardens, lawns, long showers and flushing toilets. Most Australian states are now worried about not having enough water, and there are more and more restrictions on how much we're allowed to use. The Murray River no longer gets good flows of melted snow in spring, something which is blamed on global warming and climate change.

Scientists agree that climate change is caused by increased levels of carbon dioxide, mainly from burning fossil fuels for energy. Humans have to find other solutions to making energy, such as using the wind and the sun, because the main 'solution', desalination, won't help. You need energy to get salt out of water, and we get energy by burning more fossil fuels. The best guess is that climate change means that Australia will be much drier in the future, that there'll be less rain. We need to get used to being water smart—or to starving!

Perhaps we should all start having bucket showers to save water.

Coping with thirst and heat

Travelling into the centre of the driest continent for long periods meant spending a summer there. That meant living in terrible heat. Charles Sturt sheltered in an underground room that he and his party had dug out to escape the high temperatures.

Thirst was bad, but dehydration was worse. Dehydration means your body does not have as much water and fluids as it should and if it's severe, you can die. In hot dry weather, you can lose a lot of water through sweating and your mind can become confused. Henry Bryan, a young Englishman, probably died of dehydration after he was separated from Governor Gawler's party in 1839, not far from the Murray River. He'd left his clothes behind, which suggests he was delirious. He'd been carrying an English compass, but the needle of an English compass often jams in the Southern Hemisphere, thanks to something called magnetic dip. Because he was suffering from dehydration, he was probably too confused to realise that he needed to tilt his compass to get an accurate reading. Whatever happened, his body was never found.

Frederick Smith, another young Englishman, was unlucky enough to go out with George Grey, a fool who entered dangerous territory without any training or experience. Smith died of thirst, struggling along beaches north of Perth. He'd declared that he was exhausted and couldn't go on. His companions pushed on without him, and were found by John Roe's rescue party, but when they got to Smith, he was dead.

Getting water for the horses in dry country.

PROJECT COLLECTING WATER

This project shows you how to make a solar still to collect water. It's a standard survival technique using a pit with some plants in it. The plants release water vapour, which then condenses on the plastic, runs down to the lowest point and drips off. The still works just as well with the pit filled with salt water, instead of plants. The only difference is that the water vapour comes from the evaporation of the salt water.

How to do it:

1. Dig a pit and place the plants in the bottom.
2. Put the bucket in the bottom of the pit.
3. Lay the plastic over the hole and weigh it down around the edges, first with pebbles and stones, and then with sand, so as to seal the pit.
4. Place one pebble on the plastic to make sure the lowest point is over the bucket and wait.

What else you can do:

Vary the design to find the most efficient one, publish it on the Internet and become famous!

Checklist
- a plastic sheet
- somewhere sunny where you can dig a hole
- digging tools
- some pebbles, stones and sand
- a small bucket or other container
- some green vegetation that you can cut and place in the pit

This is a pit, right? That means it's a bit like an animal trap. How will you make it safe for animals or unsuspecting people? Talk to your parents.

CHAPTER 8

TRYING TO STAY ALIVE

In 1874, Ernest Giles listed what a successful explorer had to be able to do. An explorer must 'be able to take, and make, an observation now and again, mend a watch, kill or cure a horse as the times may require, make a pack-saddle, and understand something of astronomy, surveying, geography, geology, and mineralogy'. We could add that he also had to be able to make repairs to all sorts of equipment and clothes, stay calm in the face of disaster, know how to signal for help and what to do when someone becomes ill or injured.

Francis Birtles rode his bicycle many times across Australia between 1905 and 1912. You can see the rifle he used to shoot rabbits, strapped on the front left side of the bike.

Making repairs

People who lived in the bush used the bark of the stringy-bark tree and greenhide (unpreserved animal skin) to make things, but they needed tools to work them. Horses needed new shoes on long trips, which meant taking spare horseshoes and nails, a hammer, anvil, bellows, tongs, files and more. They needed axes, saws, tomahawks, picks, shovels, a brace and bit (a tool to bore holes), a spokeshave (a smoothing tool), a chisel, an emery stone (for grinding and polishing) … the list went on and on. They usually carried spare canvas, tools to work it, wire, rope, screws, bolts and, if they carried their water in metal tanks, they took a soldering iron and solder.

Not long ago I was visiting a cemetery in Sydney and saw by chance the grave of Francis Birtles, who was described as a 'photographer and explorer' on his headstone. He died in 1941, which, as far as explorers go, is quite recent. I was curious about him and went on to discover that Birtles was more of an adventurer than an explorer. He took the first bicycle across the Nullarbor Plain and, a few years later, drove the first car across.

Birtles was very resourceful when it came to making repairs to keep his car going in the very harsh and remote country he was driving through. Occasionally, Aboriginal people's knowledge of 'bush' mechanics also came in handy. Birtles fitted the car with wooden axles (the bars that connect the wheels) because, after his bicycle trip, he knew that the risk of breaking an axle was high, and he knew that he could always make a replacement out of the local timber.

A bush mechanic uses the sap of the bloodwood tree and a hot stick to repair Birtles' car in Arnhem Land in the Northern Territory.

We are all nearly naked, the scrub has been so severe on our clothes; one can scarcely tell the original colour of a single garment, everything is so patched. Our boots are also gone.

John McDouall Stuart, 11 July 1861

Explorers obviously had to save weight where they could, so often if they needed a new piece of equipment, for example an axe handle, they'd make one. Repairs were a regular task. In 1845, Ludwig Leichhardt described how each afternoon, after setting up camp, the members would wash and mend clothes and repair the saddles, pack-saddles and packs. Eight weeks before William John Wills died, he wrote 'our clothing, especially the boots, are all going to pieces, and we have not the materials for repairing them properly'. Just after Wills died, but around 1500 kilometres away, the harsh country had also ruined the clothes of John McDouall Stuart's party.

William John Wills lies dying.

Giles, on the other hand, knew how to work with leather and thought that only leather was tough enough to last in the outback. In early 1874, he repaired his leather boots, using 60 horseshoe nails in each boot, calling them 'perfect dreadnoughts with which to tread upon any mountain'.

Any one in future traversing these regions must be equipped entirely in leather; there must be leather shirts and leather trousers, leather hats, leather heads, and leather hearts, for nothing else can stand in a region such as this.

Ernest Giles, 24 November 1873

Coping with disaster

Whatever else explorers had to be able to do, they had to manage in spite of small or large disasters. While some died, others suffered but survived, reaping a reward by having a good story to tell. Explorers wanted to find fame and great fortune. They generally missed out on the fortune, so to win fame, they needed to tell great yarns that would make their published journals bestsellers.

Three weeks after repairing his leather boots, Giles was nearly killed when his horse Diaway fell over a bank. Both horse and the rider survived, but Diaway scrambled up, leaving Giles hanging down, with one of his wonderful boots caught in a stirrup. Diaway was a nervous colt and took off, dragging Giles along with him through dense scrub and kicking out with his hooves. This actually saved Giles' life because the horse kicked him so hard that the boot tore apart and his foot came free.

Here, Ernest Giles has drawn himself being dragged along the ground by Diaway.

Ernest Giles' illustration of an accident in camp.

DID YOU KNOW ?

If you're attacked by a crocodile, fight back—with force! It will try to drag you under the water but it's useless just to thrash about. If the crocodile starts rolling and twisting, make sure that you roll and twist in the same direction (otherwise, the part of your body that's in its mouth will be torn off).

To have a chance of escaping, you have to stay calm and deliberately attack it. Poke or hit its eyes, the most sensitive parts of the crocodile, with anything you have handy, such as a stick or knife, or even your hands. If you can't get to the eyes, go for the nostrils or ears.

If the croc has your hand in its jaws, you have a problem. Experts say you should reach down into the back of its mouth and find the flap that stops water running into its throat. If you pull on this flap, water floods its lungs and makes it feel as if it's being drowned. (I'd like to shake the remaining hand of whoever came up with this idea!)

Disaster nearly happened when James Cook was sailing up the east coast in the *Endeavour* in June 1770, after leaving Botany Bay. Cook had been in the tropical Pacific and knew about coral reefs. The southern parts of the Great Barrier Reef were well out to sea, so he was more worried about the rocks on the shore. However, Cook had no way of knowing that, as he sailed north, the reefs were closer to the land and, one night, the ship struck what Banks called 'sunken coral rocks'. It started to leak and, as it was a long way from shore, the officers and crew knew they were in trouble.

Making the right decision is, of course, essential to staying alive. Cook did just this by putting midshipman Jonathan Monkhouse in charge of fixing the leak, as Monkhouse had seen how this was done on another voyage. Cook hoped to get the ship to the land, where it might be used to make a smaller vessel. In the end, the crew didn't need to do this. After making it to shore, they repaired the *Endeavour* and took her triumphantly home, complete with all their charts, scientific data and collections.

H.M. Bark *Endeavour*. In 1770, the *Endeavour* struck a coral reef and began leaking.

Staying calm

Staying calm is a part of making sure you survive. This was the case when the *Endeavour* started leaking after becoming stuck on the coral reef. Joseph Banks, the botanist on board, noted in his journal how calm everybody was. Calmness leads to clear thinking, and clear thinking leads to good decisions.

Although John Lort Stokes mightn't have known what to do when he was in danger of being attacked by an 'alligator', or as we would say, a crocodile, he remained calm. He had just stripped off to swim across a creek when a crocodile appeared in the water nearby. Crocodiles move slowly on dry land, but are faster than people in water. The tide was coming in and Stokes was on mud that would soon be covered by water. As the crocodile was waiting, Stokes knew he needed to get out of there and frantically swam to safety.

Stokes certainly knew how to make a good story out of his adventure. He always told good stories, even if some of them sound exaggerated.

Robert O'Hara Burke and William John Wills are Australia's most famous explorers, but only because their wanderings were such a disaster. Burke was not a calm man, and he repeatedly made the wrong decisions. The expedition took too much equipment (including six tonnes of firewood!), then they abandoned or dumped the wrong items along the way, including the lime juice, which would've saved them all from suffering the disease of scurvy.

My only chance of escaping the monster was to hasten back to the boat, and to cross the last creek before the alligator, who appeared fully aware of my intentions. It was now, therefore, a mere matter of speed between us, and the race began. I started off with the utmost rapidity, the alligator keeping pace with me in the water. After a sharp and anxious race, I reached the last creek, which was now much swollen . . . ; while the difficulty of crossing was aggravated by my desire to save my gun. Plunging in I reached the opposite shore just in time to see the huge jaws of the alligator extended close above the spot where I had quitted the water. My deliverance was providential, and I could not refrain from shuddering as I sat gaining breath upon the bank after my escape, and watching the disappointed alligator lurking about as if still in hopes of making his supper upon me. Waiting till the monster came close, I took a deliberate aim at his eye, which had only the effect of frightening him a little.

John Lort Stokes, 12 October 1839

While Burke and Wills and two others kept going on their expedition, some of their back-up party waited at Camp 65 on Cooper Creek. Weakened by scurvy, they left, after burying some food near the Dig Tree, just a day before Burke and Wills staggered back. Burke and Wills found the food and left a message to say that they were heading to Mount Hopeless. If they had left a clear sign carved on the Dig Tree, the back-up party who later came back looking for them would've known to dig in the same place to find their message. If Burke and Wills had stayed calm and retraced their steps to Menindee, they would all have been saved. In the end, John King was the only survivor.

A rescue party finds John King. Living with the local Aboriginal people saved his life.

Robert O'Hara Burke, William John Wills and John King staggering back to Cooper Creek in 1861.

Augustus Gregory's horse treads on an 'alligator' in Victoria River in 1856.

A Closer Look

When disaster struck the *Endeavour*

At 11 pm on 11 June 1770, disaster struck and the *Endeavour*, under the command of James Cook, ran aground on a coral reef off the coast of north-east Australia and became lodged there. The ship's hull (bottom) was badly damaged and water started pouring in. A longboat was sent out and the crew tried to pull the ship off the reef but it wouldn't budge. Next they tried to help her float free by throwing overboard six cannon, iron and stone ballast (heavy material kept onboard to make the ship stable), casks, ruined stores and drinking water. Again, they failed. Eventually, the *Endeavour* floated free on the high tide. To keep the leak under control, Cook agreed that the hole needed to be fothered when midshipman Jonathan Monkhouse (or Munkhouse) suggested it.

Fothering was a little-used method of plugging a hole using a sail that was hauled under the ship with ropes. Before doing this, the sail was filled with wool, dung from any animals aboard and oakum (tar-filled rope fibre). The idea was that the material would be sucked into the hole and stop—or at least slow—the leak. The fothering of the *Endeavour* was successful and the ship's only operating pump was able to pump out water that was still entering the hull. A week later, the *Endeavour* reached a sheltered beach where, for seven weeks, the crew stayed to repair the damage.

The Endeavour River where James Cook's ship, the *Endeavour*, was repaired after striking a coral reef.

Signalling for help

A number of explorers mention taking rockets with them, mainly to use as signals, but sometimes to scare off groups of threatening Aboriginal people. Burke and Wills certainly started out with some rockets but, like the lime juice, they abandoned them, not thinking that they'd ever need them. Even if they'd fired three gun shots, close together, in the quiet of the night as they approached the Dig Tree site, they might've been heard: three shots, three whistle blasts (three anything, in fact) are a standard signal for help in the bush.

In December 1844, Leichhardt's party knew what to do when one of their party was lost: they'd learned the Aboriginal art of the cooee.

Robert O'Hara Burke being buried.

Upon reaching the place of our next camp, Mr Roper went to cut tent-poles, but, perhaps too intent on finding good ones, unfortunately lost his way, and wandered about the bush for about five miles before we were able to make him hear our cooees.

Ludwig Leichhardt, 8 December 1844

When they became lost in the bush, Europeans called 'cooee', a signal they'd learned from Aboriginal people.

Getting medical treatment

The biggest killer was accidents followed by thirst and disease. Explorers took medical and surgical supplies with them, for both people and animals. If you were ill or hurt, you could easily die. At the end of the nineteenth century, David Carnegie carried Epsom salts (used to treat fevers, swollen and painful wounds, indigestion and constipation), carbolic oil (used as an antiseptic on wounds), eucalyptus oil (used to treat almost anything from a sore to cancer) and some beef cubes, but that was all they had. These 'treatments' were used usually without any real idea of what good or harm they might do.

Carnegie reported with some disgust that a medical orderly at Hall's Creek was planning to treat scurvy with salt beef. Carnegie was a bit of a know-all, and he insisted that the man be given some of his beef cubes, but they would've been just as useless as the salt beef.

Another disease that explorers caught was trachoma, often referred to as 'ophthalmia', though more people have probably heard of it as 'sandy blight'. This was a bacterial infection of the eyes that could make an explorer blind. Although nobody knows the truth, it's possible that this was what killed Leichhardt's lost expedition members when they disappeared, somewhere between Queensland and Western Australia, in 1848.

Lieutenant John Lort Stokes was speared in the lungs at Victoria River, 1839.

PROJECT

PUTTING TOGETHER AN EMERGENCY KIT

Successful explorers thought ahead and carried items that they might need in an emergency. When you go on a bushwalk, what do you take with you in case of an emergency?

I have been carrying the same bivvy (bivouac) bag for 30 years. Even though I've never used it, I always carry it—just in case. It's a large, tough, orange plastic bag, big enough to sleep in or put an injured person in to keep them warm and dry. One day, it may save a life. Nobody wants to carry unnecessary weight, but nobody wants trouble either.

How to do it:

Look through this list of items. To make it more of a challenge, there are a few items on the list that are less useful than others, and there might be a few items that have been left off the list.

Which would you take as emergency items for a day walk? Which would you take as emergency items for a four-day expedition?

Ask some adults which items they would take.

Emergency Kit

- a billy to boil water in
- a bivvy bag
- a compass
- a copy of a plan that shows where you will be and when (give the copy to someone before you leave)
- a GPS (Global Positioning System) receiver
- a large hammer
- a map in a sealable plastic bag
- a mobile phone
- a needle and thread
- a raincoat (it helps to keep you warm as well as dry)
- a sack from a wine cask (it can hold five litres of water, just pop the tap off, fill it and click the tap back on)
- a sleeping bag
- a small first-aid kit
- a small unbreakable mirror
- a tent
- a torch that can flash (or a camera with a flash on it)
- a two-way radio
- an umbrella
- a whistle to attract attention
- extra water
- some matches in a waterproof container
- some spare muesli bars or other energy food
- three bricks
- warm clothing
- water purification tablets

PROJECT

FINDING DISMAL PLACE NAMES

Ophthalmia was a serious problem, though Ernest Giles made light of it, calling the range of mountains that includes Mount Newman the Ophthalmia Range.

There are many gloomy and disaster-related names on the map of Australia, including Mount Hopeless, Useless Harbour, Wreck Bay, Disaster Bay, Desolation Glen and more.

How to do it:

See how many dismal names you can find using an atlas, a geography dictionary or an online reference source for Australian placenames.

Then see how many positive names you can find.

Mt Robinson
The Governor

From Ophthalmia Range no watercourses are visible
either to the east or north, the country is level to the east
no other ranges visible.

Ophthalmia Ra.

Red sand
bloodw

grow only on
sandhills.

nearly north and south.

CHAPTER 9

AN EYE ON THE WEATHER

In nineteenth-century Australia, explorers worked on the basis that the continent had four seasons a year—spring, summer, autumn and winter. It took until the 1970s for Australians to realise that much of Australia does not have the same weather pattern as Britain. We now understand that there are two weather cycles, called El Niño and La Niña, that operate across the Pacific Ocean. El Niño causes drought and La Niña brings rains. Without this knowledge, every explorer was at risk, and they needed to watch the weather closely for signs of danger by observing the barometer, looking for unusual bird behaviour, listening to frog calls, and watching for storm clouds.

Droughts

Working horses need as much as 70 litres of water a day, so water was a problem on expeditions until camels replaced horses. But camels and people still need water, even if not so much. You might think a drought was the worst time to go exploring, but Charles Sturt thought the drought of 1828 would actually give him the chance he needed to push through the Macquarie marshes in New South Wales, which, by his reckoning, would be dry.

Storm clouds over a central Australian desert.

Floods

Today, the Macquarie marshes are desperately short of water, thanks to the dryness of a prolonged El Niño event. This is made worse by farmers taking water from the Lachlan River, which drains into the marshes.

1817, however, was a year of heavy rains and the water in the Lachlan River was high. So, when John Oxley's party reached the river, it could go no further. The men couldn't make a bridge out of the large trees on the bank because they were surrounded by fast-flowing water. So, using smaller trees further away from the river's edge, they made a raft, but the strong current washed it down the river for more than a kilometre. They then moved back up the river and tried to make a bridge again. The current was so strong that each time they chopped down a tree, it fell into the river and was carried away. With the flood finally easing, they went back to making a raft and eventually got their equipment across. But that wasn't the end of their woes, as the floodwater was draining into the Macquarie marshes where it stayed, preventing Oxley, in 1818, from going any further.

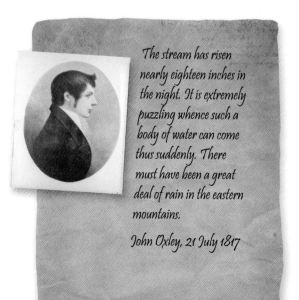

The stream has risen nearly eighteen inches in the night. It is extremely puzzling whence such a body of water can come thus suddenly. There must have been a great deal of rain in the eastern mountains.

John Oxley, 21 July 1817

Peter Warburton had a very narrow escape, on 20 December 1873, when he and his party were close to death from illness, starvation and thirst. About three o'clock in the morning, they were woken by a roaring sound, only to find that the river beside them had gone from a dry bed to a rapid stream, 300 metres across, with timber and ducks floating on it. Luckily, they'd already moved their camp to high ground because Warburton thought the wet season would arrive soon, and so they were safe. Warburton expressed his joy at going from 'draining a quart pot an hour from a sandhill under intense heat and thirst, to a quiet admiration of a gliding stream'.

The expedition party was so weak that if they'd still been camping in the river bed, they could easily have drowned. Never camp in a river bed is a good rule to follow, as I discovered once, when I was camping in a dry creek that began running in the night. We had some warning when the rain began, but Oxley and Warburton didn't have this warning because it wasn't raining where they were. In their cases, the floodwaters had come from somewhere else a long way off where it had been raining.

As Augustus Gregory learned, water could be a danger for animals on expeditions—he lost at least three of his horses to drowning, his dog was seized and drowned by a crocodile, and 11 of his sheep drowned after being left in a leaky boat. But hardly any explorers died by drowning. The only person that we know who died in this way was James Taylor, one of Major Mitchell's party, in 1836. The disappearance of many minor explorers could've been due to drowning, but we can't be certain.

The disappearance of Ludwig Leichhardt in 1848 is still a mystery. He and his equipment seemed to have disappeared without trace, as did all of the iron work his men had with them, such as tent pegs, billy tripods and the frames of the pack saddles. It's possible that Aboriginal people had found and taken the iron work away. The best theory of where he died is based on the discovery, in the early 1900s, of a damaged gun hanging in a tree, which indicates that he died somewhere between the Tanami and Great Sandy deserts. The rusty gun was thrown away and only its name plate survives. It was only in 2007 that researchers at the National Museum of Australia confirmed that the plate had probably belonged to Leichhardt. Ernest Giles had a theory that Leichhardt's disappearance could have been caused by the flooding of the Cooper River.

When Ludwig Leichhardt disappeared, another expedition was organised to search for him.

Explorers and their horses had to wade through flooded forests, like this one. The horses were at risk of drowning.

Strong winds

The wind and weather mattered to explorers, both on land and at sea. Wind from the wrong direction could bring fire rushing across the plain. At sea, winds could threaten to push anchored ships onto rocks or reefs and, in 1819, Lieutenant Phillip Parker King and his crew had to set sail in the middle of the night in a strong wind because they only had one anchor, which wasn't enough to stop them from being pushed towards a reef.

Some ships didn't survive rough seas and ended up as shipwrecks.

Explorers were in great danger of being ambushed by fires.

PROJECT   MAKING A WIND VANE

Wind vanes show us the exact direction of the wind, something that's important in a sailing vessel, or if a fire's approaching. This wind vane hangs by its balance point, which is towards the front, thanks to the weights attached to the front end. When the wind blows, it finds more surface behind the balance point, so the tail of the arrow is away from the wind. The arrow points to where the wind's coming from, not to where it's going.

How to do it:

1. On the cardboard, draw an arrow, 30 cm long.
2. Tape a coin to each side of the arrow near the head.
3. Use a pin to find the balance point where the arrow hangs level, by pushing the pin through and trying to find the right place.
4. Make the pinhole larger and tie the cotton thread through it.
5. Test your wind vane by walking around carrying it by the thread. It should always point where you're going.
6. Hang your wind vane in a place where the wind isn't funnelled or channelled by or between buildings.

What else you can do:

1. Can you make a reliable wind vane with just a thread of cotton?
2. Why do you think pelicans fold their long necks back on their bodies when they fly? It's because if they didn't do this, the wind would catch their large beaks and bend their heads around to point backwards, like a wind vane. The flying reptile, the pteranodon, didn't fold its neck but it did have a skull crest to balance wind effects on its beak. If it hadn't had a crest, wind forces on the beak would've pushed its head around and its neck would've snapped.

Checklist
- light cardboard, such as a manila folder
- pencil
- ruler
- scissors
- two 20 cent pieces or two heavy steel washers
- sticky tape
- a pin
- some cotton thread

When you're testing out your wind vane, watch where you're going so that you don't bump into anything.

A Closer Look

El Niño and La Niña

You often hear people mention El Niño and La Niña on weather forecasts or in discussions about droughts, floods and extreme weather events. But what do these terms mean and why are they important to our climate here in Australia?

Strangely enough, Australia's weather is strongly affected by events on the other side of the world. In the early 1500s, fishermen along the coast of Peru knew about a current of unusually warm water that came ashore usually every three to seven years around Christmas time. They named the current El Niño meaning 'the boy' (that is, the Christ child) because of its Christmas connection. This current usually meant bad fishing.

We now know that this current affects Australia's weather and world weather. Normally strong trade winds blow from the east along the equator pushing water into the Pacific Ocean. These winds result in surface water being warmer on our side of the ocean and the sea level being a little higher. When the trade winds weaken or even reverse, warm water is swept to the South American side of the ocean. The warmer water temperature changes the weather of the region, increasing clouds and rainstorms. Meanwhile, on our side of the Pacific, we tend to experience drought and bushfires.

Another climate change term La Niña ('the girl' in Spanish) is regarded as the opposite of El Niño. It refers to significant cooling of the central and eastern Pacific Ocean. In Australia (particularly eastern Australia), La Niña events usually mean an increased chance of rain.

Scientists are working on improving their predictions of El Niño and La Niña events. Advance knowledge of reliable long-term weather conditions would enable farmers to reduce planting and animal herds in preparation for drought periods.

Cold and heat

In sunny Australia, could cold ever be a threat? The earliest explorers certainly didn't think so, but Watkin Tench found it extremely cold in July 1791 when he and William Dawes reached the George's River, south-west of Sydney. Even back in Sydney, people complained of the cold that night but, out in the bush, the two officers were amazed. In central Australia, the temperature can go from 40°C by day to 0°C at night if the sky is clear, so wherever they went, the explorers needed shelter and warmth.

Most of the explorers had more of a problem with heat. In 1845, Charles Sturt and his party dug an underground room so that their pens wouldn't dry out so fast when they were drawing charts. In the end, they used it as a shelter for almost ten months.

Some explorers, such as those in the Burke and Wills expedition, beat the heat by travelling at night and sheltering during the day in whatever shade they could find.

... we started at about half-past seven, and were lucky enough to find a creek with some water in it about ten miles on, where we remained until evening; for it is dry work travelling in the middle of the day, with the thermometer varying from 90 to 105 degrees in the shade, and about 140 degrees in the sun. Well, we started again in the evening and walked until between nine and ten P. M.; and again at three A. M. and pushed on until midday. We then went on from five P. M., as before, until nine P. M.; and then from two A. M., and reached the camp at nine A. M., having walked more than eighty miles in rather less than fifty hours, including sleeping, feeding, and all stoppages.

William John Wills, 4 December 1860

Drops of water on a tin pot, not altogether out of the influence of the fire, were frozen into solid ice in less than twelve minutes. Part of a leg of kangaroo which we had roasted for supper was frozen quite hard, all the juices of it being converted into ice.

Watkin Tench, 18 July 1791

Early explorers couldn't get weather reports, like we do, from television, radio, mobile phones or the Internet. They had to rely on all the clues that nature provided. That meant looking at the clouds, the wind and the temperature. They knew, for example, cool winds from the nearest sea are likely to mean rain. In the far north of Australia, it also meant looking at the calendar because the wet season always arrives as summer starts.

A barometer could also give warning, because a drop in air pressure often indicates rain. There were also other 'barometric' clues. When the barometer drops, many fish stop biting, frogs start calling as much as two days before the rain starts, and a number of bird species stop calling, while a few change their calls.

Sometimes it was too hot to travel during the day.

CHAPTER 10

SHELTERING IN TENTS

The first tent in Australia was probably set up by shipwrecked sailors who knew how to make a shelter by hanging a sail over a branch of a tree or over a rope. Heavy canvas tents were common in the earliest days of Sydney. In 1803, Nicolas Baudin's French crews, who were visiting Sydney in two ships, set up tents near Sydney Cove, close to where Macquarie Street is now.

An exploring party, looking for suitable country for sheep, relax outside their tent.

Ludwig Leichhardt outside his tent, about 1846.

Tents set up along the eastern shore of Sydney Cove by the crews of French explorer Nicolas Baudin in 1803.

Wherever they went, explorers needed shelter for themselves and for their stores and equipment. They usually made camp before dark, so they needed shade and shelter, if it rained. Still, many like Thomas Braidwood Wilson were prepared to rough it and did without tents. On an expedition in Western Australia in 1829, Wilson described how the party members rolled themselves in blankets next to a fire to sleep at night. (Apart from being an explorer, Wilson sailed nine times to Australia as a surgeon on convict ships, and he brought the first hive of bees to Australia. The New South Wales town of Braidwood was named after him.)

Most explorers used tents. Some of these were no more than a fly—a sheet of canvas or other material that could hang over a rope between two trees. This would keep most of the rain off and stop some of the wind, if it faced the right way, but it wouldn't stop the mosquitoes getting in, or small marsupials, usually referred to as 'rats' and 'mice', from attacking the food stores. In 1860, the Burke and Wills expedition had to leave Camp 63 on Cooper Creek, mainly because there was a plague of rats and the only way they could keep them from eating their food was to hang the stores in trees.

These men are going to sleep under the stars, rolled in blankets next to their campfire.

The crew of HMS *Porpoise* lived in tents on a sandbank for seven weeks after the ship was wrecked on a reef in August 1803.

I may here describe the usual method of encampment on such expeditions. A convenient spot being selected, if possible, to windward of a large fallen half-burned tree, a few branches and bushes are placed in a semicircular form, as a defence against the night wind; the log is kindled, and soon forms a blazing fire, which, being too fierce for cooking, a smaller one is used for that purpose. After supper, each rolls himself in his blanket, and, with his feet towards the fire, soon falls asleep.

Thomas Braidwood Wilson, 1835

Herschel Babbage's lightweight tent in 1857. This tent is ingenious because all he had to carry was the tent itself. He would've cut the three forked sticks and the long pole from local timber.

Flies covering a pack on a horse's back.

Most people complained about the mosquitoes and flies, even in what is now the Sydney suburb of Homebush. In the 1840s, Homebush was a wilderness, far enough out for bushrangers to prowl. One woman complained about the flies, writing that they 'swarm in every room in tens of thousands, and blacken the breakfast or dinner table as soon as the viands [dishes of food] appear, tumbling into the cream, tea, wine, and gravy with the most disgusting familiarity'.

So, you can imagine how difficult it was to escape pests out in the bush. In early 1829, Charles Sturt tried rolling himself in a waterproof 'boat cloak',

but he perspired so much that his clothes became soaked and he had to stand next to the fire in the morning to dry them. A member of his party, Hamilton Hume, who couldn't bear being wrapped up, suffered the consequences and was dreadfully bitten all over by the mosquitoes.

When Sturt was exploring again in December 1844, the mosquitoes came close to causing a disaster. In the middle of the night, the tarpaulin on John Jones' dray caught fire. Jones was a bullock driver and he normally slept in the dray. That night, he'd put smouldering cow dung under the dray so that the smoke would drive off the

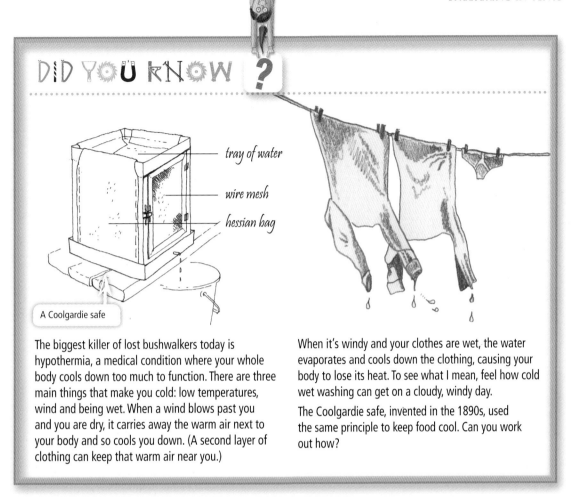

DID YOU KNOW ?

tray of water

wire mesh

hessian bag

A Coolgardie safe

The biggest killer of lost bushwalkers today is hypothermia, a medical condition where your whole body cools down too much to function. There are three main things that make you cold: low temperatures, wind and being wet. When a wind blows past you and you are dry, it carries away the warm air next to your body and so cools you down. (A second layer of clothing can keep that warm air near you.)

When it's windy and your clothes are wet, the water evaporates and cools down the clothing, causing your body to lose its heat. To see what I mean, feel how cold wet washing can get on a cloudy, windy day.

The Coolgardie safe, invented in the 1890s, used the same principle to keep food cool. Can you work out how?

mosquitoes, but the tarpaulin caught fire. The medicine chest was scorched, two bags of flour were damaged, and Jones lost most of his clothes.

Even sheltering in the shade of a tree could bring problems, as John Lort Stokes and his companions discovered while on the southern side of Melville Island in August 1839. The tree had green ants in it, and Stokes reported that the men were 'jumping like madmen'. They named the place Ant Cliffs after the experience.

Still, however basic they were, tents gave the best portable shelter, and what the explorers lost on weather-proofing (when they used only a single layer of material instead of two), they gained on lightness. When Watkin Tench described his travels in April 1791, he referred to his tent as a 'wigwam', showing how the first settlers used familiar American terms to describe things that were new to them. (Other American terms that they used included 'Indians', 'creek' and 'bushrangers'.)

A Closer Look

Surface tension

Water is peculiar stuff. In fact, chemists tell us that, at temperatures that humans can live at, water should be a gas!

There is a reason why water isn't a gas at those temperatures and that's because water molecules attract each other very strongly. This means that when you have a drop of water, the molecules pull towards each other, forming a spherical drop.

Of course, if it's a falling raindrop, the wind rushing past pulls the drop out into a tear-shape, and if it's a drop that's sitting on a greasy plate, gravity pulls it down into a squashed sphere.

Left to itself, with no other forces pulling on it, water contracts to have the smallest surface area possible, thanks to the way water molecules pull each other together. Water resists having its surface area increased, and that is what lies behind the old trick of 'floating' a greasy pin on a glass of water.

This also explains why some insects can 'walk on water': if an insect is light, it can't stretch the surface of the water enough to break through it. Scientists say that the surface shows 'surface tension'.

Detergents and soaps are 'wetting agents' that work by having one end of the molecule that attracts water, while the other end attracts other things. This stops that water molecule attracting other water molecules, reducing the surface tension. The result is that the other forces can take over, and the water clings to whatever it is supposed to 'wet'.

It's surface tension that stops water flowing through a tent roof. But, if you touch the roof from below, the force you use makes a channel through the canvas and the water can flow through without having to change its surface area. In other words, the effect of surface tension stops working.

When John Horrocks went exploring in South Australia in August 1846, he soon found out how flimsy his tent was when his goats, which he'd taken with him for meat, started climbing and jumping on the tent and tearing it. Still, said Horrocks, goats were better than sheep because 'they give tongue immediately they are caught, so that the natives could not take any without being heard'.

If Horrocks objected to Aboriginal people taking his goats, he didn't mind taking *their* food animals.

He had a large dog that often caught emus and, being a well-bred and educated Englishman, he was keen to collect specimens. That enthusiasm, combined with Harry the camel, killed him and became the reason why we know what tents looked like in the 1840s. The story on the next page tells you why.

Harry was the only camel in the colonies, the last to survive from a small shipment sent to Australia from the Canary Islands, but nobody in Australia knew how to handle these unfamiliar animals.

Horrocks' goats and camp site. The main tent looks rather like a 'wigwam'.

When camels were brought out in larger numbers in the 1860s, Afghans were hired to manage them and to teach Australians how to manage them as well, but Harry was alone, with men who didn't understand camels, so he became very bad-tempered. One day, Harry grabbed one of the goats and tried to break its back and then bit Garlick, the servant, leaving serious wounds on both sides of his head. But worse was to come, a month later.

One of the party, a man called Kilroy, saw a new and interesting bird, and told Horrocks. Scientists back then killed their specimens with fine shot that wouldn't damage the specimen. Because Horrocks' double-barrelled muzzle-loader was loaded with heavy shot, he needed to reload it with fine shot. He was in a hurry, so he stood close to Harry who had the shot belt slung over him, but the camel lurched to one side and the gun went off. Horrocks lost two of his fingers and the heavy shot entered his jaw, knocking out some of his teeth. The artist Samuel Thomas Gill was there and used a handkerchief to stop the wounded hand bleeding.

The other men put Horrocks in his tent, leaving Gill to look after him, and headed off to bring back a horse to carry him home. To pass the time, Gill painted a number of watercolours, including ones of the tent, which is why we have a record of what tents looked like in the 1840s.

Horrocks died of gangrene from his wounds, a month after the accident.

Gulnare the dog keeps Samuel Thomas Gill company outside the tent in which the wounded John Horrocks lies. Harry the camel, of course, is unaware of the trouble he's caused.

PROJECT   MAKING A TENT

The army and new arrivals in the colony of New South Wales used big heavy canvas tents but you're going to make one that's small and light enough to carry. Here's some information to help you.

A simple tent will keep out the rain, so long as there are two layers of cloth: a tent underneath, with a stretched sheet, called the fly, over it.

Raindrops will splash through the fly fabric, but only as tiny droplets that will run down and off the sloping fabric of the tent. (A fly over a tent breaks up the big drops.)

If you touch the inside of the tent, water will start to drip through. So your tent needs to be wide enough and high enough to let you lie down and sit up without touching the tent with your head or shoulders.

If the slope isn't steep enough, water won't run off, the material will get wet, and water will start to drip through.

Rain can probably blow in at about 45°, so the tent needs to be long enough to keep your head (or feet) dry if the wind changes in the night—unless the tent has door flaps.

A steep tent will shed water more efficiently, but if it's too steep, it uses too much material and weighs too much.

How to do it:

Look at the picture to see how to make a tent and a fly using the materials in the checklist. If you are planning to leave the tent up for a while, use some thick material to protect the tree trunks from the rope.

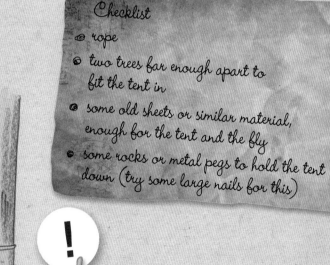

Checklist
- rope
- two trees far enough apart to fit the tent in
- some old sheets or similar material, enough for the tent and the fly
- some rocks or metal pegs to hold the tent down (try some large nails for this)

!

Parents can get a bit upset about holes in good sheets! You, on the other hand, will be upset by holes in you, made by not being careful enough with nails or pegs.

On his expeditions across Australia in the early twentieth century, Francis Birtles set up all sorts of shelters and tents.

CHAPTER 11

MEASURING DISTANCE

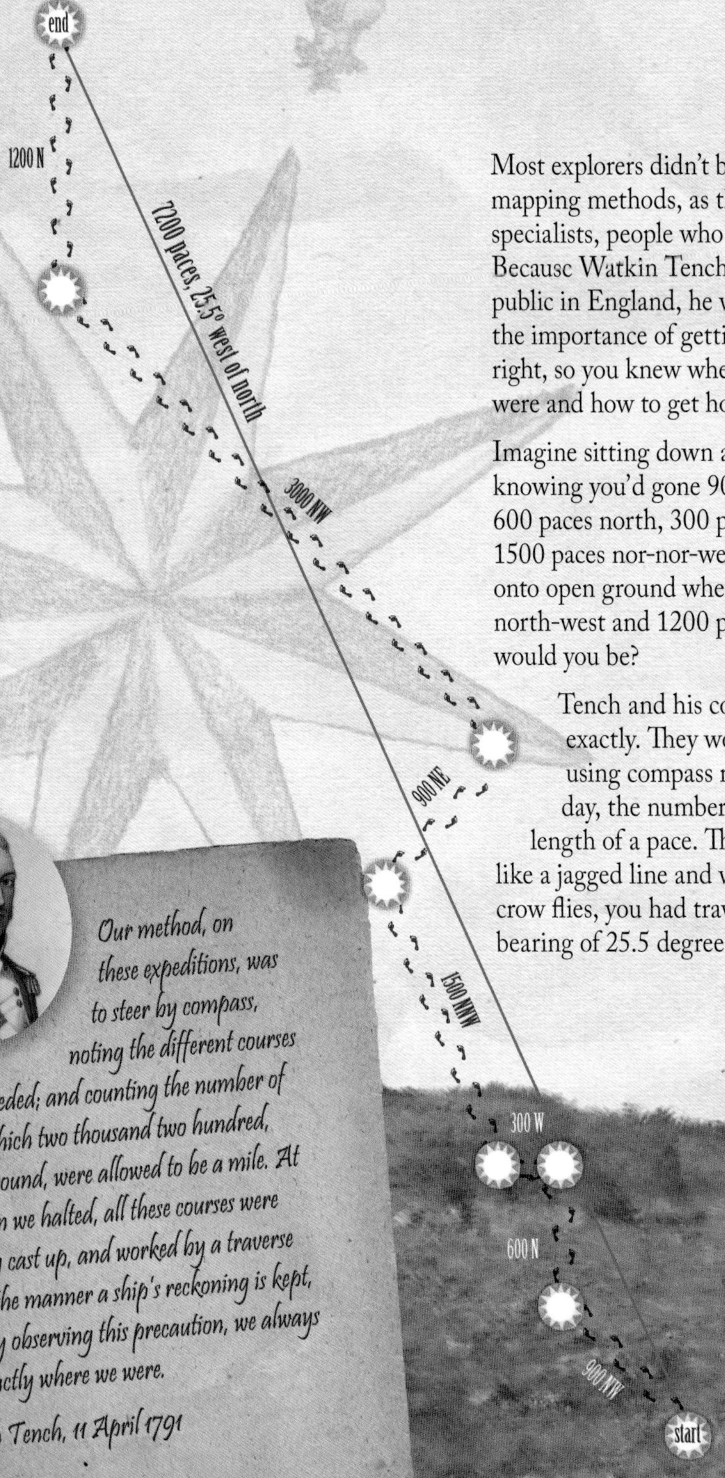

end

1200 N

7200 paces, 25.5° west of north

3000 NW

900 NE

1500 NNW

300 W

600 N

900 NW

start

Most explorers didn't bother to explain their mapping methods, as they were writing for specialists, people who already knew the details. Because Watkin Tench was writing for the general public in England, he went into more detail about the importance of getting distances and directions right, so you knew where you had gone, where you were and how to get home again.

Imagine sitting down at the end of the day, knowing you'd gone 900 paces north-west, 600 paces north, 300 paces west under a cliff, 1500 paces nor-nor-west, 900 paces north-east, onto open ground where you covered 3000 paces north-west and 1200 paces due north. Where would you be?

Tench and his companions would've known exactly. They would've drawn a diagram using compass readings taken during the day, the number of paces walked and the length of a pace. The diagram would've looked like a jagged line and would've revealed that, as the crow flies, you had travelled about 7200 paces on a bearing of 25.5 degrees west of north.

Our method, on these expeditions, was to steer by compass, noting the different courses as we proceeded; and counting the number of paces, of which two thousand two hundred, on good ground, were allowed to be a mile. At night when we halted, all these courses were separately cast up, and worked by a traverse table, in the manner a ship's reckoning is kept, so that by observing this precaution, we always knew exactly where we were.

Watkin Tench, 11 April 1791

PROJECT   PACING DISTANCES

How to do it:

My home is on a main road, and the odometer in my car tells me that the traffic lights at the main shops are 1.1 kilometres from my front door. On the way, I pass an oval where there is a 100-metre running track marked out. If I turn left, I can find an Olympic swimming pool that is 50 metres long and 25 metres wide, so one circuit of the pool is 150 metres. So I have a lot of ways of measuring how many paces I do in 100 or 1000 metres.

We can also use good scale maps to measure street distances. And, to measure walking tracks from a map when the track wiggles around, you need a good scale map and a piece of cotton thread or wool. Put the cotton along the track on the map and then stretch it out over the map scale. Walk each of these marked paths several times, using comfortable strides, and record the pace counts. Calculate the number of paces you take to walk one kilometre. You're now ready to measure some distances.

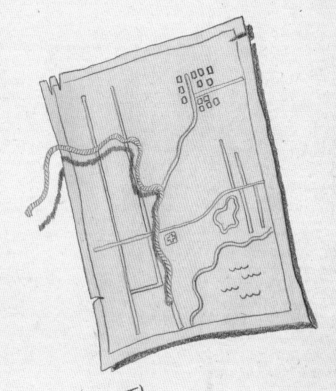

What else you can do:

Use a pedometer to see whether the pace count or distance shown matches your calculation.

You can count while you are walking, but be really careful when crossing roads.

Measuring a ship's speed at sea

Marine speed and wind speed are both measured in knots. A speed of one knot means travelling through the water at the rate of one nautical mile (6000 feet or 1852 metres) per hour. The name of the unit comes from the old trick of tossing a 'log' overboard on the end of a knotted line, and seeing how much line runs out as the log sits there and the ship sails on.

If you ran the line out for an hour and three nautical miles of line went into the water, then the ship was travelling at three nautical miles an hour. The snag was that it'd take a long time to haul all the line back in again. The solution was to scale everything down to a manageable size. The sailors took a sample of just 60 seconds, one minute or 1/60th of an hour.

Each 1/60th of a nautical mile of line, 100 feet (30.5 metres), that runs out during a minute indicates a speed of one nautical mile per hour. As the line had a knot tied in it every 100 feet, the sailors just counted the knots as the line ran out and reported 'three knots' as the speed, if that was the number of knots they saw and felt.

Using the chain and perambulator

From about the 1830s, a metal chain was used to measure distances. The chain was made up of 100 metal links and was 22 yards (about 20 metres) long. The men who did the measuring were called chainmen and they used the chain just as we would use a tape measure to measure a long jump. If the chainmen went up or down a slope, they noted the angle so corrections could be made and, if part of the chain was stretched out over a creek, a correction was used to allow for the extra distance caused by the curve of the sagging chain. In the 1870s, surveyors started using a steel tape, which they preferred to the chain, as it was in one continuous piece. It was also lighter and so didn't sag as much, and it could be wound up in a coil, making it easy to carry.

A 20-metre surveyor's chain made up of 100 metal links used to measure distance in the 1860s.

The crew on this ship is winding in the line after tossing a log overboard to measure the ship's speed.

Two members of Sturt's party using a surveyor's chain to measure distance in the dry country of central Australia.

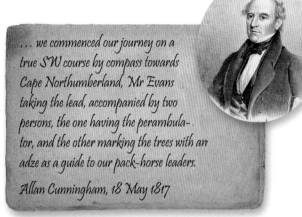

... we commenced our journey on a true SW course by compass towards Cape Northumberland, Mr Evans taking the lead, accompanied by two persons, the one having the perambulator, and the other marking the trees with an adze as a guide to our pack-horse leaders.

Allan Cunningham, 18 May 1817

Chaining was used mainly to measure an accurate baseline. For everyday work, when the measurements didn't need to be as exact, a perambulator was enough. The proper name for a baby's pram is 'perambulator', but a surveyor's perambulator was a measuring wheel with a way of recording the number of times the wheel turned. Only Allan Cunningham mentions it being used, in Oxley's 1817 expedition on the Lachlan River, but it's likely that other expedition parties also used it.

The perambulator was not entirely reliable and, in August, Cunningham described their day's march as '13¼ miles per perambulator but only 12½ on our true course'. This explains why the later military men, like Major (later Sir Thomas) Mitchell and Captain Sturt preferred the chain. In 1845, Sturt reported that the chainmen had kept up with them and 'chained 61 miles on a bearing of 55 degrees to the west of north' in open country.

George Evans, the first surveyor to cross the Blue Mountains, New South Wales, and map the other side, was a bad speller. He wrote of 'a river lett' when he meant a rivulet, a small river, and his superiors in Sydney and London poked fun at him and looked down on him. So Evans was not allowed to lead any more expeditions, but he was welcome to go out as Oxley's second-in-command. Oxley knew how lucky he was to have such a skilled surveyor, and left Evans to do a lot of the trail-finding.

Even today, Evans' misspelling of 'rivulet' can be seen on the road sign (left), west of the Blue Mountains. His mistake is less obvious in the river name (right) because, somewhere along the way, 'River Lett' has been reversed to 'Lett River'.

PROJECT
MAKING A MODEL PERAMBULATOR

How to do it:

1. To make the wheel, use the compass to draw four circles, each with a 32-centimetre diameter, on the cardboard. Cut them out and glue them together.

2. Cut three long pieces of wood and one short piece. Drill a five-millimetre hole at the end of two of the long pieces. Glue the pieces together to make a fork.

3. Make a hole through each cork or piece of foam and through the centre of the wheel. Push the dowel through one cork, then through the wheel and through the other cork. Glue the corks to the wheel and dowel.

4. Near the rim of the wheel, glue a folded piece of card. Then tape the rim.

5. Hammer a nail to the inside of one of the prongs of the fork about 14 centimetres above the centre of the wheel. Insert the wheel between the prongs.

6. As you run the perambulator along the ground, you'll hear the click of the card against the nail for every revolution of the wheel. Your perambulator clicks every metre.

Now you're ready to measure some distances, such as in your local park.

Checklist
- thick cardboard
- a compass
- 5 mm dowel
- pieces of wood
- two corks or pieces of round polystyrene foam
- glue
- a nail, a hammer, a drill
- masking tape

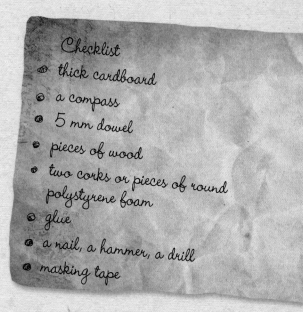

long piece of wood ——
short piece of wood ——
nail ——
long piece of wood ——
dowel ——
cork ——
cardboard layers ——
folded card ——

DID YOU KNOW ?

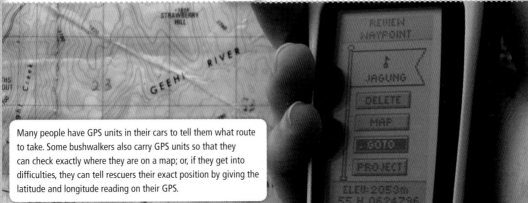

Many people have GPS units in their cars to tell them what route to take. Some bushwalkers also carry GPS units so that they can check exactly where they are on a map; or, if they get into difficulties, they can tell rescuers their exact position by giving the latitude and longitude reading on their GPS.

During World War II, radar was developed mainly to measure the speed and range of enemy aircraft and ships. After the war, it was thought that surveyors could use radar to measure distances between two places, but it was not accurate enough.

In the late 1950s, a device called a tellurometer was developed that used microwaves to measure distances more accurately than surveyors could with a chain and theodolite. Today, surveyors use a device called a 'total station', which is based on the tellurometer idea, using microwaves or infrared. Some of them can also use GPS (Global Positioning System) data (see page 132).

Although they aren't accurate enough for commercial surveys of property, ordinary GPS units can plot the start and end points for field trips, and any points on the way that a person chooses. The GPS can even generate a route map.

A flat steel tape used to measure distance from the 1870s and on, even into the 1960s. It was an improvement on the chain as it could be wound up and easily carried.

A perambulator, or surveyor's wheel, was pushed along to measure how far it was from one place to another. To calculate the distance, it had a dial attached to it that took readings of the number of times the wheel revolved and the user then multiplied this number by the circumference of the wheel.

A Closer Look

How does GPS work?

At any time, day or night, there are 24 satellites circling the earth in six circular orbits. They're 20 200 kilometres above the surface of the planet, travelling in six different paths. Each orbit takes 12 hours, and from any place on the ground, there'll always be at least six satellites 'visible'. You might see them at night with a telescope if the sun is in the right place, but the satellites are too small to see with the naked eye.

There are a number of monitoring and control stations around the world. These track the satellites and pass accurate information back to them. Because each satellite 'knows' where it is and where it's going, it can transmit very accurate time signals and position signals. This satellite navigation system is known as a GPS or Global Positioning System.

Each GPS unit (a device that receives the satellites' signals) listens to four of the available signals and uses the time delays between the various signals to calculate its exact position, speed and time. The time delay is the same as a distance. We're able to plot a position on a map when we know our exact distance from three fixed points. With the satellite data, the time delays give us exact distances from a number of satellites, and so provide a solution.

When we use a GPS unit for on-road navigation, we combine it with a map to provide information on where we are, usually with a voice advising us when to turn. The system uses a database for calculating routes, alternative routes and corrections to cover mistakes.

In the outback, away from any roads listed in the database, the main use of the GPS unit is to calculate accurate positions, and that sort of database will usually draw a rough map, with any selected points marked. With no compass, no notes and no trouble, you can later retrace your steps to within a few metres, or draw a map of your route.

Estimating distance

Sailors knew how to estimate how far off a gun was by counting the seconds from the flash of the gun to the time when the bang was heard. Each six-second delay meant that the gun was one nautical mile away. Lieutenant Grant recorded this way of measuring distance in the log of the surveying vessel, the *Lady Nelson*, in Victoria's Western Port in late March 1801. Barrallier and Murray waited until 8 pm to fire the guns, probably because it was quiet and calm at that time of the day and also because it was easier to see the flash of the gun when fired at night rather than the gun's puff of smoke in the daytime. They fired four guns—one for attention and three more to get an average count. Today, we estimate the distance of lightning in the same way, by counting the seconds between a flash of lightning and the sound of thunder, with three seconds meaning one kilometre.

Sometimes, it was enough to say that a mountain appeared to be 50 miles (about 80 kilometres) away, or that a river was about 200 yards (about 183 metres) across. Clarke the Barber, the convict who lied about the Kindur River, probably went a bit too far when he said that he was uncertain if the Kindur was 500 miles (about 800 kilometres) or 5000 miles (about 8000 kilometres) long, but most of the explorers could make a good attempt at estimating distances.

Barrallier and Murray went on shore ... ascertaining the different points of this harbour that were in sight; at 8 pm fired four guns by the request of Mr Barrallier, in order to measure a base line.

Lieutenant James Grant,
26 March 1801

HMS *Lady Nelson*

PROJECT — ESTIMATING DISTANCE BY SOUND

You'll need a thunderstorm, a bit of patience and a view out of a window.

How to do it:

Watch for a flash and then count the seconds: one second is about the time it takes to say 'a thousand and one'. So count like this: 'a thousand and one, a thousand and two, a thousand and three', and so on. You can practise this while watching the second hand of a clock until you get it right. Then time the gap between lightning and thunder. Remember that three seconds indicate a distance of one kilometre.

PROJECT — THE THUMB MEASURER

How to do it:

To work out how far away something like a hut is, hold your hand at arm's length with the thumb upright. Look through your left eye and line your thumb up with the hut. Then change eyes and look through your right eye: your thumb will appear to have moved sideways. Estimate how far it has moved. Let's say it moved to a spot, eight metres away from the hut. Then multiply your estimate (in this case, eight metres) by nine to get the distance. So the hut is about 72 metres away.

What else you can do:

Estimate the height of a tree by changing the height to a distance along the ground.

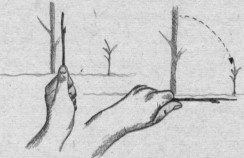

In this bush method of estimating the time to sunset, one finger equals 15 minutes of sun remaining.

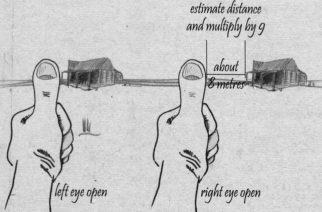

estimate distance and multiply by 9

about 8 metres

left eye open   right eye open

45 minutes to sunset

90 minutes to sunset

CHAPTER 12

MAPPING

Today's maps are usually accurate drawings of pieces of land, where all the angles, directions and distances on the maps match those on the ground. Most maps also have other information, such as the steepness and height of the land, tracks and paths, rock types and plant cover, and how the land is used. Producing accurate maps needs careful measurement and recording.

Nowadays, mapmakers begin with aerial photographs or satellite images when creating their maps, but explorers had to work from the ground and imagine what an area would look like from above—in other words, a bird's-eye view of the land.

There were a few basic principles that everybody agreed on in the nineteenth century. The planet was more or less spherical and it turned once every 24 hours, while the sun and the stars stayed where they were, so they could be used as reference points. A grid of latitudes and longitudes could be drawn to locate a place, just as I can locate my house in square C2 of map 174 in my street directory.

They also knew that the earth had a magnetic field that made freely moving magnets point north and south. This allowed navigators to point their ship in a particular direction.

A grid is a useful way to locate a place: a street map is divided into squares (you have to imagine the grid lines on many street maps); a map in your atlas has a grid of latitudes and longitudes.

Mapping from the sea

Maps of the coast were based on sketches, notes and sightings of peaks, headlands and other features that were taken from onboard a ship. While an artistic member of the crew sketched the coastline, others recorded the compass bearings, the ship's direction and its speed, and water depth. Later, these bits of information would be put together to make a chart.

Sailing ships usually couldn't stop and wait while mapmakers made their charts. Today, ships and boats have engines, so they can stop where they want to, but sailing ships only went where the winds and currents took them. If currents or winds went the wrong way, navigators mightn't even be able to get close to the land they wanted to map. Ships, for example, had to stay clear of shores if the wind was blowing towards the land, to avoid putting the vessel in danger. Mapping from a distance meant an island might be mistaken for a headland, or an inlet might be missed. Later charts were more accurate, as you can see from two charts of Rottnest Island (off Fremantle, Western Australia), drawn 150 years apart.

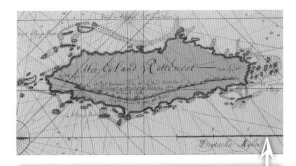

The 1697 map of Rottnest Island (above) is not as accurate as the one drawn in 1841 (below).

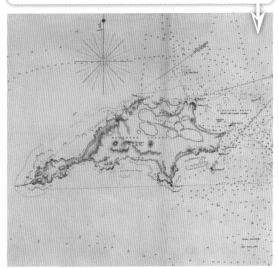

From this map of Abel Tasman's course in the 1640s, you can see that he hadn't discovered that Tasmania and New Guinea were separate from the mainland of Australia. Charts were engraved by artists, who liked to add ships, mermaids, spouting whales and other decorations that you wouldn't see on modern maps. The radiating lines are called wind roses, and they were used for navigation.

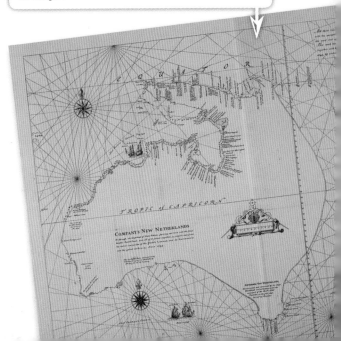

The entrance of Oyster Harbour, King George III Sound, Western Australia in 1825. Explorers usually had a few places that they returned to, where they knew the locals were friendly, they knew where to get water and, most importantly, they had measured the position very accurately.

The junction of the Murray and Darling rivers in 1860. Sketches like this were also made on land expeditions to help later visitors check their position, just as coastal sketches were made and published to help later navigators in the same way.

The view of Descartes Island in Western Australia, painted by explorer Phillip Parker King, who surveyed parts of the Australian coast from 1817 to 1822 in the ship, HMS *Mermaid*.

Compass used by explorer David Lindsay during his explorations, 1879.

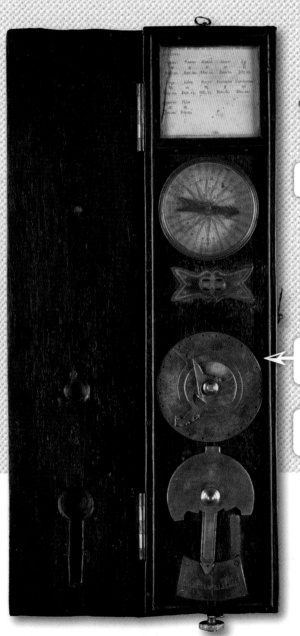

This wooden box belonged to Captain James Cook. It contains a set of instruments: a table of star signs and dates, a compass, a spirit level, a sundial, an astrolabe and a measuring instrument.

Compass, sundial and geographical clock, about 1780. The outer circle of the geographical clock lists 51 cities and locations around the world, including Botany Bay and Norfolk Island.

A Closer Look

This 1830 map uses Mercator's projection in which Greenland looks much larger than Australia even though it's just over a quarter of the size.

What's a 'good' map?

A 'good' map means different things to different people. To mapmakers, a good map is one on which you can measure distances. The world is a sphere but, since the sixteenth century, mapmakers have usually represented it as a flat rectangular map, like the world maps you see in atlases, using what's called 'Mercator's projection'. Mercator maps show all of the parts of the world and how they relate to each other. But something happens when you try to take the surface of a sphere and lay it flat—parts of the world near the north and south poles get stretched, so that Greenland, for example, looks much bigger than Australia, when in fact it's just over a quarter of Australia's area. This, however, doesn't matter because you can look at it on a globe and see it as it really is.

Bushwalkers have a different idea of a 'good' map. They carry sketch maps on which you can't measure distances. But nobody needs to—the number of metres is less important than how long it takes to get somewhere. The time isn't on the printed map, but bushwalkers write that information on their own copies. A sketch map is not to scale and, if there are three gullies and you need to go up the middle one, that part of the map is magnified to make the details clear.

This sketch map distinguishes between well-used tracks that you can follow and other ways that you can go, called 'negotiable ways'. The dashes show tracks and the dots show other ways. Notice the two gullies on the western side of Crow Hill and see how you need to go up the second gully. These gullies are made larger on the map to make this clear.

The Horizontal Waterfalls, north of Broome, Western Australia, are created where a large area has only a narrow opening to the sea and the huge tidal range makes the water rush out as the tide falls and rush back in as it rises. In the nineteenth century, sailing ships could be destroyed in seas like this.

Surveying with small craft

In the early nineteenth century, the only sort of boat that could travel in the opposite direction to the wind was a rowing boat. Later, from the 1830s, there were steamships, which had steam-driven engines, but these were too weak and inclined to break down at the wrong time when Australia's coasts were being mapped.

Still, people could see that the age of steam was coming, and a lot of work was done, mostly in small and bobbing boats, finding safe channels in the sea and marking shallow patches of water and hidden rocks. This would make future steam navigation around Australia's northern coast much safer in seas where coral reefs might suddenly loom in front of a ship.

In Australia's north-west, where tides could go up or down by eight or nine metres in a few hours, there could be tremendous currents and captains needed to know this or their ships would be destroyed.

This vessel, the *Tom Tough*, was used in Augustus Gregory's expedition in the 1850s. It was typical of the smaller craft that were used in survey work.

By the late 1840s, charting unknown waters had become an art. In late 1846, a captain in the Royal Navy named Owen Stanley was ordered to take HMS *Rattlesnake* to Australia, to survey the area around Hervey Bay in Queensland for a new settlement. The settlement never happened, but he carried Edmund Kennedy's expedition to Cape York, and he mapped parts of the coasts of New Guinea and northern Australia, aided by the schooner *Bramble* and a 'decked boat' called the *Asp*, as well as smaller boats and dinghies and 190 officers and men. (A decked boat is one that was small enough to be lifted onto a ship, but large enough to have a deck for shelter.) As well as the threat of bad weather and strong currents, another problem for the crews of small boats was that they couldn't see very far. Ships and boats working together kept the crews safe in storms because a large ship had lookouts, high on the ship's masts, from where the crew could see distant landmarks, while the boats could manoeuvre close to the shore where the crew could see the fine details.

The surgeon and naturalist on the *Rattlesnake*, John MacGillivray, wrote a book about the voyage of the ship and left us with a clear description of how Stanley and his crew surveyed the waters.

HMS *Rattlesnake*

DID YOU KNOW ?

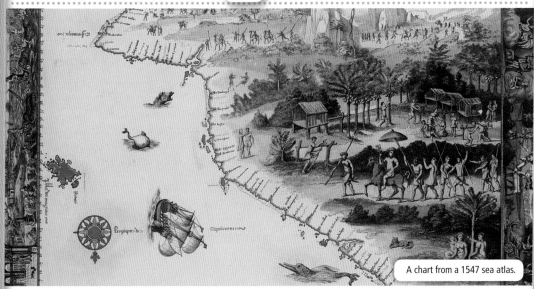

A chart from a 1547 sea atlas.

For some people, maps have a fatal attraction. They will take risks or pay other people large amounts of money to take risks, just so that they can steal and own maps that are old and beautiful. If the maps are in books, they tear them out, often damaging the books and spoiling the maps in the process. These people are vandals. Miles Harvey tells the story of one map thief in *The Island of Lost Maps: A True Story of Cartographic Crime* (2000). If you read it, you'll understand why libraries ask you to read old books in a supervised area!

Lieutenant Dayman, in the Asp, laid down the coastline and neighbourhood as far as the next station twenty or thirty miles in advance. Lieutenant Simpson with the pinnace [a smaller boat accompanying the Asp] continued the soundings several miles further out, both working in conjunction, and often assisted by another boat ... The Rattlesnake in shifting from place to place, aided by boats in company, sounded the centre of the channel, usually following one of the lines run by Captain P. P. King, and marked upon his charts.

John MacGillivray, 26 May 1848

On 6 May 1848, the *Rattlesnake* was at anchor near Dunk Island in the Great Barrier Reef while Captain Stanley and another officer used a theodolite, an accurate angle measurer, to measure angles on the main landmarks, in order to work out the ship's position. Crews, rowing around in boats, took 'soundings' to find out how deep the waters were. To do this, they lowered a heavy lead weight on a line into the water until it hit the sand or mud below. The line had marks on it that told them the water's depth.

Making deductions

The later surveyors often found that, once the crew of a small boat could make a closer inspection, a landmark that earlier surveyors had identified as a headland turned out to be an island, while some reported 'islands' were actually headlands. Sometimes, when the weather and the seas were dangerous, explorers had to make deductions, or guesses, and sometimes those deductions were wrong.

By 1798, the British Government complained about the lack of progress in making a profit from Australia. Sir Joseph Banks asked how 'a body of land, as large as all Europe, does not produce great rivers capable of being navigated into the heart of the interior'. If people could find such a river, he thought, they could reach more of Australia and have a better chance of finding riches—and the river *had* to be there! All the rain had to flow somewhere, and so there must be a giant river that would carry boats to the centre of the continent. The Rhine and Danube rivers in Europe, the Congo and Nile in Africa, the Amazon in South America and the Mississippi in North America just *had* to be matched by a large river in Australia. However, the surveys of the coast of Australia didn't lead to the discovery of any giant rivers. In northern Australia, the Ord is a mighty river in the wet season, but the wet season brings cyclones that are dangerous to ships, so there were no explorers there to see the river flowing out to sea.

When no big rivers were found, people began to talk about the possibility of an inland sea. They came to this conclusion because they didn't understand Australia and assumed that it was the same as Europe.

Australia's a very large, flat and dry continent. It gets less rain than European countries and most of it doesn't pour down to the sea, but trickles along,

Like this surveyor from the past, today's surveyors use theodolites to measure angles between points and so work out distances. A theodolite sits on top of a tripod and has a small telescope.

evaporating as it goes. In south-eastern Australia, much of the water in the huge Murray–Darling river system runs into sand, billabongs, swamps or wetlands before it gets to the sea, and sandhills hide the mouth of the Murray River. More water evaporates than reaches the sea.

The myth of an inland sea continued. When Matthew Flinders saw the high cliffs of the Great Australian Bight on Australia Day in 1802, he wondered if the cliffs could be a dam wall, holding back a great sea of fresh water. Almost 40 years later, Edward John Eyre saw that there was no dam.

But Eyre made an error of his own when he looked down from the northern end of the Flinders Ranges in South Australia. In all directions, he saw lines of trees along the banks of riverbeds. The streams spread out and, from what he could see, each of them ended in the same lake, which he decided was impassable and so blocked any passage to the north. This made him decide to walk west, in the hope of finding a way into the northern interior. In fact, the lake was a series of lakes and Eyre could've found his way between them if he'd

done more investigating, but he made a reasonable decision, and went to look for a way around the barrier.

A few years earlier, in 1831, Major Mitchell, the Surveyor-General of New South Wales, was fooled by a yarn that came from a convict called George Clarke, or 'the Barber', about a giant river. Clarke had joined some Aboriginal people and lived by spearing settlers' cattle. When the police caught him, Clarke told the authorities about a grand river

These coastal views were painted in 1791 and show the south coast of Tasmania (top), Botany Bay (middle) and the entrance to Port Jackson (bottom) in New South Wales.

This is the coastal view of cliffs of the Great Australian Bight, on the edge of the Nullarbor Plain. In 1802, Matthew Flinders wondered whether an inland sea lay behind these cliffs.

called the Kindur that flowed, always to the north of west, until it reached a seashore. He probably hoped to avoid punishment with his tale. Mitchell liked the idea and went searching for the river, but never found it.

As late as 1845, Charles Sturt hoped he had proved there was an inland sea after he showed pictures of animals in a book to some Aboriginal people in central Australia. One man seemed to recognise some of them and have names for a seahorse, a turtle and other marine fish. The witness called some of the other fish *guia*, which Sturt thought might be the equivalent of the English word for 'fish', but he thought that if they knew the names of *some* marine animals, they must've been to a sea, either the ocean or an inland sea.

One thing was certain: making deductions was a good starting place, but in the end, the only answer was to go, to look and to make an accurate map.

Mapping on sand

The 'mud map', a rough guide scratched in sand or mud, is an old tradition among European Australians. It leaves out the unimportant parts and sometimes exaggerates the important details. The original Australians drew mud maps long before Europeans settled in Australia in 1788. Explorers increased their knowledge of surrounding areas by getting Aboriginal people to draw maps of their country. In 1876, this was how Ernest Giles found out where the Ferdinand River ran in central Australia.

A map drawn with a stick on the ground is good enough for getting from one place to another, but not good enough for making accurate maps that will last. The problem was that accurate maps needed accurate instruments, and those were often heavy to carry.

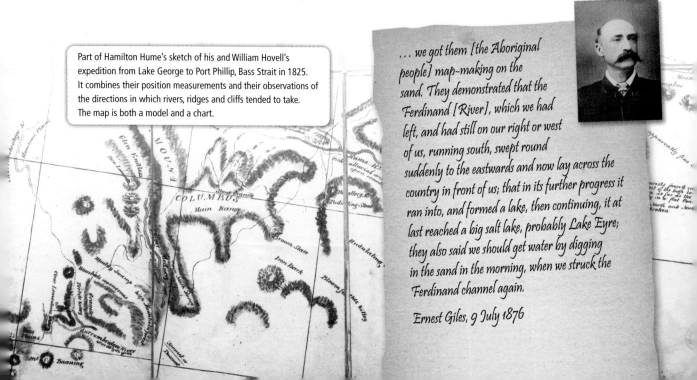

Part of Hamilton Hume's sketch of his and William Hovell's expedition from Lake George to Port Phillip, Bass Strait in 1825. It combines their position measurements and their observations of the directions in which rivers, ridges and cliffs tended to take. The map is both a model and a chart.

... we got them [the Aboriginal people] map-making on the sand. They demonstrated that the Ferdinand [River], which we had left, and had still on our right or west of us, running south, swept round suddenly to the eastwards and now lay across the country in front of us; that in its further progress it ran into, and formed a lake, then continuing, it at last reached a big salt lake, probably Lake Eyre; they also said we should get water by digging in the sand in the morning, when we struck the Ferdinand channel again.

Ernest Giles, 9 July 1876

Ships swing around and rock and bob, but at least they can carry the heavy items that an explorer needs when making accurate maps of the coast from the sea. It wasn't so easy for land explorers who couldn't always carry the heavy, and sometimes fragile, measuring instruments and who often had to make do with lighter, less accurate ones.

A compass is still the best way to get rough directions. It's just a long magnet that swings until it lines up with the earth's local magnetic field. Most of the time, it will line up north–south, but

John Oxley had some problems in August 1818, in the Warrumbungle ranges of New South Wales. His compass went wild, and he named the hill he was on Loadstone Hill, after loadstone (or lodestone), an old name for a magnetic mineral that distorts the reading on a compass. Captain Cook had similar problems on Magnetic Island.

Captain James Cook's ship, the *Endeavour*, below decks. Notice the amount of stowing space for equipment, food, water, and plant and animal specimens.

There were two parts to exploring: the first part was understanding the bush, the second was being able to navigate and draw good maps. Hamilton Hume was an excellent bushman, and William Hovell, a former sea captain, knew how to use surveying and navigation instruments, but he didn't know a lot about the bush. Between them, they made a good team.

There were two main skills for mapping (or three, if you include not getting lost!): one was measuring angles and distances so that a small area could be plotted on paper, and the other was getting precise positions and directions from the stars (rather than from compasses, which could vary if there were magnetic rocks about).

This is part of John Oxley's chart, drawn on an expedition in the interior of New South Wales between 1817 and 1820. It includes Loadstone Hill which caused the compass not to work properly because of magnetic material in the hill. On the chart, Oxley wrote compass readings, the heights of many places and notes about the country. He also used shading to show hills and slopes.

In this project, you'll make a compass by taking a magnetised pin, putting it on a disc of cork and floating it in a glass that's very full of water.

For this project, you need to know a little bit about water. When you put water in a glass, the surface is not flat. It's lower in the middle because water and glass attract each other. When you put a piece of cork in a glass of water, it moves slowly to one side and up the slope, and then sticks in one place and won't turn. This is no use to us. The good news is that water also attracts water. When a glass is really full of water, the surface bulges up above the top of the glass, so that now the highest part of the water's in the middle, and the cork will stay in the middle.

How to do it:

1. Magnetise the pin by holding it and stroking it, from point to head, with one end of the magnet.

   Usually, after 40 or 50 strokes, it'll start to be magnetised, but you always need to go the same way, and you need to move the magnet away as you go from the head back to the point to start again. You can test the pin to see if it's magnetised by moving it near another steel pin that's hanging from a long cotton thread. When it's magnetised, it'll attract the other pin.

2. Cut a slice off the cork. (Be careful or ask an adult for help.)

3. Place a glass of water on a level surface. Using the jug of water, slowly fill the glass until the surface bulges up just above the lip of the glass.

4. Place the magnetised pin on the cork and place it gently on the water. Watch as the cork and pin turn to line up with the earth's magnetic field.

Cutting cork with a sharp knife can be dangerous! Be careful.

PROJECT

MAKING A COMPASS

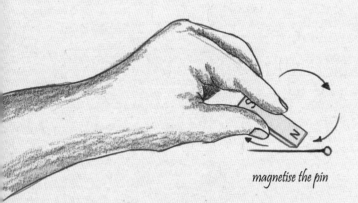

magnetise the pin

Checklist

- a bar magnet
- an iron pin (test the sewing kit with a magnet to find a pin that'll work!)
- one glass
- some water in a jug
- a cork from a bottle or a piece of polystyrene foam
- a sharp kitchen knife
- a cutting board

What else you can do:

As you'll know, this kind of compass wouldn't be much use to explorers—see if you can come up with a more portable design!

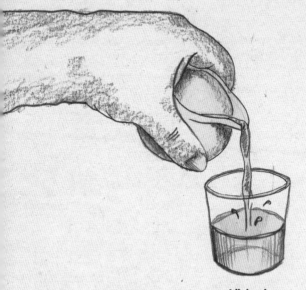

fill the glass

place the cork and the pin on the water

watch as the cork and pin turn to line up with the earth's magnetic field

PROJECT   FINDING NORTH FROM A SHADOW

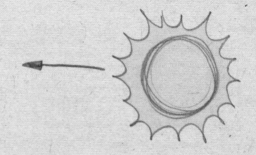

As the earth turns, the sun appears to move across the sky, and while a morning shadow is to the west, noon shadows point south, and later afternoon shadows point east.

How to do it:

1. Put the stick in the ground so that it's upright, and place a pebble at the end of its shadow.

2. Every five minutes, place another pebble at the end of the stick's shadow. Around the middle of the day, the shadow of the top of a tree or the tip of a stick moves from west to east, and even 15 minutes of observation will give you an accurate east–west line. And once you know this, you can find north.

You'll find that it gets shorter then, after a while, it starts to get longer again. When the shadow's at its shortest, it's pointing due south. If you miss the shortest point, find two equal lengths either side, and take their average, by drawing a line halfway between the two directions.

Checklist
- *some pebbles*
- *a pen*
- *a straight stick*
- *a place in the sun around midday with some shelter from the wind.*

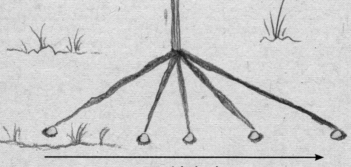

W   *movement of shadow direction*   E

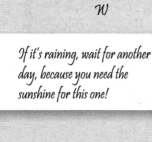

If it's raining, wait for another day, because you need the sunshine for this one!

Plotting the shadow of the tip of a vertical stick.

PROJECT FINDING THE SOUTH CELESTIAL POLE FROM THE STARS

In the Northern Hemisphere at the equinox (about 21 March and 22 September, when night and day are the same length all over the earth), the pole star would be immediately above you when you were at the North Pole. When you watch it from there (or other places), all the other stars appear to revolve around it.

There's a similar place in the Southern Hemisphere, but there's no visible star there. We call the empty central place the South Celestial Pole. Here's one way to find it.

How to do it:

1. Find the pointers (two stars called Alpha Centauri and Beta Centauri), and imagine a line joining them.

2. Now imagine a second line cutting that first line in two at right angles (if you want the fancy name, it's called the perpendicular bisector). The South Celestial Pole is where that line meets the line coming out of the bottom of the Southern Cross.

What else you can do:

To find south, imagine a line dropping down the sky from the South Celestial Pole. South is where that line meets the horizon. Note that this is true south, which is not always the same as magnetic south, which varies from place to place.

Checklist
- *a place where you can see the Southern Cross and the southern horizon and where it is safe to stand at night (Talk to an adult about the best place to go.)*

CHAPTER 13

NAVIGATING BY THE STARS

line of longitude

line of latitude

The latitude and longitude grid applied to the earth: notice how the latitude lines stay the same distance apart, while longitude lines come together.

When I was a boy, it was hard to see how mathematics was useful, especially when the mathematics I did always seemed to be impossible sums about men who cut wood with saws that had 1729 teeth per perch and were 25.6 inches long, with the saw operating at 173 furlongs per fortnight and each tooth producing one scruple of sawdust per millisecond! Sometimes it's still hard to see how that sort of mathematics is useful but navigation is one place where it is *very* important.

For thousands of years, humans looked up at the stars and wondered. Slowly, as civilisations grew, the Egyptian priest-astronomers learned to tell the time of year from the stars and to even predict the arrival of the annual floods that came down the Nile River. They also used the stars to line up their pyramids with the main compass points.

Later, navigators learned to use stars to find their way in the Mediterranean Sea (explorers in the deserts also used them to find their way). In the Pacific Ocean, Polynesian navigators made use of the stars and many other clues to sail from island group to island group on long ocean voyages.

When we compare the old navigators with modern navigators, there is one big difference—they were finding their way to where they wanted to be, *but they didn't know where they were to start with!*

To fix places on a map, you need a grid, like the grid in a game of 'battleships' or the map of a

shopping mall, where you find out where the shop you want is located at E5 (or wherever). A geographical map has a grid of the lines of latitude and longitude. To use this kind of map, navigators had to be able to measure angles and tell the time accurately.

Navigators used an instrument called a sextant to measure angles. With a sextant, they could see how far a star rose above the horizon at its highest point, and then work out their latitude (how far north or south of the equator they were). Other angles plus accurate time and some complicated mathematics indicated how far east or west of their starting place they were. That told them their longitude, allowed them to fix their position on the map and showed them which way to walk or sail to get home.

Thousands of years ago, Egyptian priest-astronomers used the stars to line up their pyramids with the main compass points.

Longitude

Sydney, Adelaide and Perth are all on about the same latitude, which means they are about the same distance from the equator. Latitude is easier to calculate than longitude. Navigators talk about 'meridians of longitude'. These are lines that join places on the globe from which you can 'see' the sun (or a particular star) at the same place on an east–west scale.

Imagine we are both in different countries but on the same latitude and talking by telephone. You can see the sun setting and I can see it right above me. That might be confusing, but then we realise that we are separated by 90 degrees of longitude, and I am 90 degrees west of you.

If you sail away from your home port with an accurate clock, you might get to a point where your clock says it's noon at home, but you can see the sun just rising. That means you are 90 degrees west of where you started out. Some hours later, you will see that it's sunset at home, but the sun is overhead where you are.

If only we had accurate clocks, said the old navigators, we could set them before we left port and so always know the time at home. So, wherever we were, at midday, when the sun was directly above us, we'd check the time on the home clock and know how far east or west of home we were by comparing the two times. In the 1700s, good clocks were only just beginning to be developed, so people needed another way to find out the time at their home port.

Map of Australia, 1866. The latitude and longitude grid, flattened as it normally appears in a map of Australia. A place can be accurately added to the map if the exact latitude and longitude are known.

Some time before he died in 1665, Sir Kenelm Digby invented a 'sympathetic powder' to cure wounds by putting it on the weapon that had caused the wound, not on the wound itself. He said that when a bandage from a wound was placed in a basin of the powder, the wounded person felt pain.

In 1687, an unknown person suggested giving each ship a wounded dog. It would travel on the ship while a bandage from the dog remained in the home port. Each hour, day and night, somebody in the home port would take the bandage, and dip it in the sympathetic powder. On the ship, the dog would yelp, telling the crew the time back in the home port. This gives a whole new meaning to 'watchdog'!

This makes a good yarn, but Digby's powder and the wounded dog methods would never have worked.

The mathematical professor at Padua hath discovered four new planets rolling about the sphere of Jupiter, besides many other unknown fixed stars [and] that the moon is not spherical but endowed with many prominences [he shall either be] exceeding famous or exceeding ridiculous.

Jupiter's moons

One of the best ideas for finding an accurate time came from an Italian scientist called Galileo Galilei, who looked at Jupiter through a telescope and saw the four largest moons of Jupiter regularly disappearing and then reappearing again on the other side (we say that they were being 'eclipsed')— *as regular as clockwork*!

Actually, in those days, clocks were so bad that Galileo would never have compared the moons with clocks, but he knew that all over the earth, navigators would see Jupiter's moons disappearing and reappearing at exactly the same time. So even if your clock wasn't very good at keeping time, all you needed was a table of when the eclipses were due, using the home-port time. Then you could calculate a longitude on the nights when there were no clouds to block the view through a telescope.

Sadly, the moons of Jupiter were hard to see from a ship that was pitching, tossing and rolling. Besides, all the masts, sails and rigging often got in the way. But, you could observe Jupiter from the land, so when James Cook wanted to fix the longitude at the Endeavour River in north Queensland, while his crew was repairing the ship, he sat down on dry land and used the moons of Jupiter to calculate a longitude, four nautical miles (7.5 kilometres) west of present-day Cooktown.

Sir Henry Wotton (1568–1639), English ambassador to Venice, sent the first news to England about Galileo's discovery of four new moons.

A Closer Look

Why is navigation complicated?

The key to good navigation is all about triangles and accurate angle measurers. To get a correct reading of something's position, you need very accurate measurement of angles, and then of distance. Imagine that you can see a number of mountains from where you are standing. If you measure out a straight line on the ground (called AB on the diagram below right) and then you measure the angle bearings of a mountain peak (called P) from each end of the line, you can draw a triangle which shows the baseline and mountain P on a map. You don't have to have been to mountain P to take these measurements. Then, you take bearings on four other mountains (Q–T) and add them to the map, even if you haven't been to them.

Locating a position on the ground means getting an accurate measure of the angle that goes from you to a selected star and to the horizon. The same instrument that is often used to take angle bearings, the sextant, can also be used to take sightings on a star or on the sun. There is just one snag: the axis of the planet is tilted and, as the earth moves around the sun, that tilt stays the same, which among other things, causes the seasons.

The tilt of the earth means that if you measure your latitude by the same star on 21 December and 21 June, there will be a difference of 47 degrees in the result! Luckily, it became possible, after about 1500, to calculate tables that show the correction you need to apply on a particular date, but that required the invention of mathematics, printing and quite a lot more.

When you take a sighting, you can draw an arc on the map and know that you are somewhere along that arc. A second sighting, using a different star, gives a second arc, and where the two cross is your latitude. Most navigators took a third sighting, just to make sure that all three arcs crossed at one place. If they didn't cross, more work was needed!

P is the first mountain plotted onto the map using the baseline AB. Then four other mountains, Q–T, have been added.

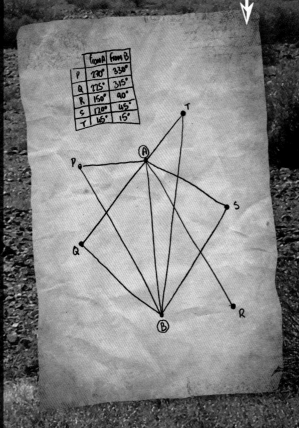

DID YOU KNOW ?

This chronometer was the first experimental marine timekeeper made by John Harrison between 1730 and 1735.

On 22 October 1707, four British warships ran into the Scilly Isles and sank because of a mistake in longitude. More than 2000 men died. Back then, there was a lot of guesswork in navigation, and the ships' navigators guessed wrongly. Everybody was horrified and, in 1714, the British Parliament passed the Longitude Act, offering a prize of £20 000 for a way of finding longitude at sea.

The best solution was an accurate clock (or chronometer). English clockmaker John Harrison started working on a new design in 1736, but he worked very slowly. By the 1760s, his first models were working, but he never received all of the prize money. Harrison chronometers were so expensive that, for a long time, even in the nineteenth century, ships relied on the method of 'lunars' to measure longitude.

A crew member using a sextant, a navigational instrument which had a system of mirrors to reflect the sun and to measure how high it was above the horizon. The sextant allowed him to work out a line of position on the earth's surface. By using other lines of position as well, the navigator could determine the ship's exact latitude and longitude.

Thomas Mitchell used this sextant during his expeditions in the 1830s to 1840s.

Lunars

Cook also used the very difficult
method of 'lunars' to calculate
longitude, and so did Ludwig
Leichhardt and Charles Sturt.
To understand this method,
you need to know that the
moon appears to move past
the star field by about
12 degrees each day.
As the moon appears
to cover an angle of
0.5 degrees, that means
the moon 'moves across
the sky' one moon
diameter each hour.
If you know where
the moon should be at
midnight in your home
port, and you see it in
the same position at 5 am
local time, you are 5/24
of the way around
the world, which means
a longitude difference of
75 degrees.

Photograph of the moon taken with the Great Melbourne
Telescope when the moon's 'age' was 9 days 0 hours, 1880s.

PROJECT   OBSERVING THE MOON'S MOVEMENTS

Sailors could use the moon for navigation as they knew that the moon 'moved across the sky' one moon diameter each hour. They worked out where they were by comparing the position of the moon in two different places.

In this project, you'll observe the 'movement' of the moon across the sky.

How to do it:

You need a night when there's a bright star, two or three lunar diameters away either east or west of the moon (although you can do almost as well with a star that's out to one side). Then all you need to do is to observe the moon's position every half an hour for two hours or more.

What else you can do:

You may like to experiment with photography. This will mean getting help from an adult who has a digital SLR (single-lens reflex) camera and who knows how to operate it. Remember that it doesn't matter if the moon's overexposed, but a shot's no good if you can't see the star, so practise with a few bright stars first, and learn what exposure you need. Ask an adult to help you with tripods and slow exposure times, because you won't get anywhere with a handheld phone camera!

midnight   *1 am*   *2 am*

CHAPTER 14

WHO ARE THE EXPLORERS NOW?

The explorers of the eighteenth and nineteenth centuries were very different from the men and women of today who make new discoveries while having all the advantages of modern technology. Unlike the early explorers, these men and women are scientists who don't have to suffer the physical hardships caused by ignorance of the harsh environment. The explorers of the past often risked their lives in a country they knew little about, and many died as a result.

In 2006, Australia celebrated 400 years of European mapping, beginning with Willem Janszoon, captain of the small Dutch ship, the *Duyfken*, who mapped part of the Gulf of Carpentaria, Queensland, in 1606.

By chance, the Gulf of Carpentaria was also where, in 2005, scientists found a large and uncharted coral reef, while other scientists in the south published maps and images of the Murray canyons, a series of huge chasms in Australia's continental shelf and slope, which had been cut by sediments and sediment-laden water flowing down the continental slope and out of the Murray River in past times. These canyons go twice as deep below

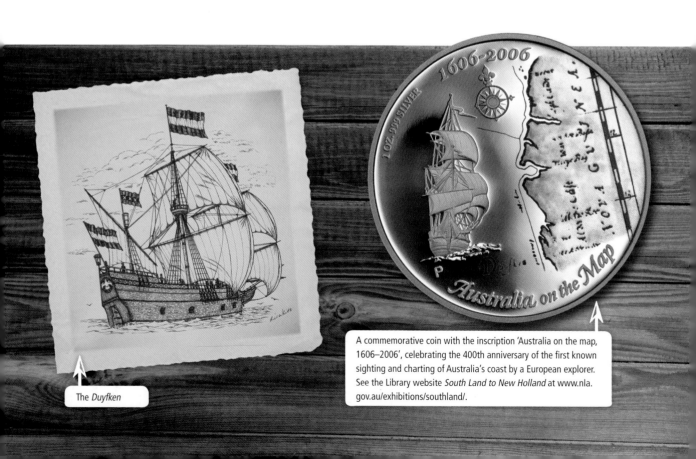

The *Duyfken*

A commemorative coin with the inscription 'Australia on the map, 1606–2006', celebrating the 400th anniversary of the first known sighting and charting of Australia's coast by a European explorer. See the Library website *South Land to New Holland* at www.nla. gov.au/exhibitions/southland/.

the sea surface as Mount Kosciuszko rises above it. Just a year earlier, in 2004, oceanographers found that the Leeuwin Current, which flows around western and south-western Australia, actually goes all the way to Tasmania, after starting at Northwest Cape in Western Australia, rather than just dying away.

In 2002, scientists began mapping the geology that lies beneath the sediments of the Murray River plain. The goldrush of the 1850s in Victoria produced 2500 tonnes of gold (two per cent of all the gold in the world today), but geologists suspect that there may be twice that amount hidden below the sand and silt, and they began mapping the rocks below the surface.

Just as I started writing this chapter, an email arrived from a friend, with a file attached that showed a satellite picture of a beach north of Sydney with curious patterns in the sand. We'll probably need to go to that beach to have a close look, but I could already see from the picture where the access tracks were. The early explorers would never have dreamed that finding a way so easily would be possible.

The Mount Alexander gold diggings in Victoria in 1853. Is there still more gold to be found there?

The Murray canyons (shown at the bottom of the image) lie as deep as five kilometres below the surface of the Southern Ocean off the South Australian coast. Although discovered after World War II, they weren't explored until 2003. A team of Australian and overseas scientists sampled the strange creatures that inhabit the dark depths of the underwater canyons and took cores of sediment up to 35 metres long that will tell us something about the history of the Australian climate.

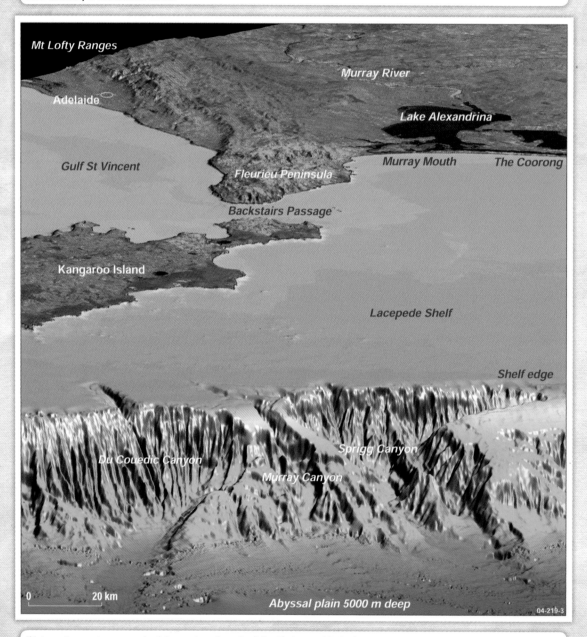

This image is computer-generated and shows a three-dimensional view. The image of the land areas was created using data from satellites. The image of the canyons was created using data collected from a ship, with advanced sonar equipment which can map the seabed very accurately.

Dr George Morrison walked alone from the Gulf of Carpentaria, Queensland, to Melbourne in 1892–1893.

Francis Birtles was an extraordinary cyclist who, by 1912, had cycled around and across Australia several times. He then swapped his bicycle for a car and, by 1927, he'd driven across Australia more than 70 times. This might sound easy but, in those days, there were no proper roads like we have today.

Francis Birtles and his dog camped beside the car, Arnhem Land, Northern Territory.

Would we call today's scientists 'explorers'? I suspect that we wouldn't. Maybe yesterday's explorers were more like the 'adventurers' of more recent times—people who've challenged themselves in an extreme way and have put their survival at risk in the process. These adventurers include George Morrison, who walked alone in 1892–1893 from Normanton, just south of the Gulf of Carpentaria in Queensland, to Melbourne on roughly the same route as Burke and Wills.

Australian adventurers aren't just men. There've been many women too, such as pioneer aviator Mrs Lores Bonney, who in 1933 was the first woman to fly solo between Australia and England. In 1977, a woman called Robyn Davidson trekked alone across the deserts of Western Australia with her dog and four camels. In 1988, Kay Cottee became the first woman to sail solo around the world without stopping.

In 1933, Lores Bonney flew her DH60 Gipsy Moth, *My Little Ship*, from Australia to England, becoming the first woman to make this solo flight. She had no radio with her and only a compass for navigation.

Being an adventurer can often be dangerous. Andrew McAuley was a rockclimber, mountaineer and sea kayaker who completed many successful expeditions. Tragically, in 2007, while kayaking between Australia and New Zealand, his kayak capsized. But McAuley had lived for adventure and died doing what he loved. Australian mountain climber Lincoln Hall was luckier. When descending from the summit of Mount Everest in 2006, he suffered from altitude sickness and his companions were forced to leave him on the mountain, apparently dead. The next morning, he was found alive by another mountaineering team. Nobody could believe that he'd survived a night in freezing conditions without proper equipment and clothing and without an oxygen bottle.

So, what would you rather be—an explorer like those from the past or an adventurer like those of today?

In 2006, mountaineer Lincoln Hall lost several fingers to frostbite when he was on Mount Everest, left for dead. If you look at his hand closely, you can see that the tops of his fingers are missing.

List of projects

169

List of images

Chapter 1

page 2
James William Giles (1801–1870)
The Departure of Captn Sturt, August 1844 (detail)
hand-coloured lithograph; 35.8 x 53.2 cm
National Library of Australia
Pictures Collection, nla.pic-an7350668

page 3 (left)
Unknown artist
Explorer Camping for the Night 1800s
watercolour on card; 32.8 x 25.0 cm
National Library of Australia
Pictures Collection, nla.pic-an21031978

page 3 (right)
Greg James (b.1954)
John Septimus Roe 1990
bronze; 193.0 x 80.0 x 60.0 cm
Courtesy of Greg James

page 4
Unknown artist
Governor Philip Gidley King from a Miniature in the Possession of his Grandson, the Hon. P.G. King, M.L.C. 1960s
colour photomechanical print; 21.7 x 14.0 cm
National Library of Australia
Pictures Collection, nla.pic-an9631735

page 5 (top)
Unknown photographer
Portrait of Henry Angel Who Accompanied Hume and Hovell to Port Phillip 1800s
b&w photograph; 11.4 x 7.7 cm
National Library of Australia
Pictures Collection, nla.pic-an22592649

page 5 (bottom right)
Unknown artist
The Hume and Hovell Expedition
reproduced from Cassell's *Picturesque Australasia*, vol. 3, edited by E.E. Morris
(London: Cassell & Company, Limited, 1890, p.173)

page 6 (top)
Walter G. Mason
Medal Given by Sir C. Fitzroy to Jackey Jackey, Native Servant to the Explorer Mr Kennedy 1857
wood engraving; 7.5 x 9.9 cm
National Library of Australia
Pictures Collection, nla.pic-an8008625

page 6 (bottom)
Samuel Thomas Gill (1818–1880)
Explorer and Aboriginal Guide c.1850
watercolour; 14.3 x 23.0 cm
National Library of Australia
Pictures Collection, nla.pic-an2377144

page 6 (bottom, inset)
Charles Rodius (1802–1860)
Bungaree, Chief of the Broken Bay Tribe, New South Wales 1830?
hand-coloured lithograph; 15.0 x 17.5 cm
National Library of Australia
Pictures Collection, nla.pic-an8953978

page 7 (top)
Unknown photographer
William Landsborough with His Native Guides Jemmy and Jacky c.1862
b&w photograph; 8.6 x 5.8 cm
National Library of Australia
Pictures Collection, nla.pic-an10570995

page 7 (bottom)
Unknown artist
Eyre's Journey to Albany
reproduced from *Illustrated Australian News*, 1 January 1891, p.12

page 8 (top)
Paul Hardy
A Positive Nuisance
reproduced from Cassell's *Picturesque Australasia*, vol. 3, edited by E.E. Morris
(London: Cassell & Company, Limited, 1890, p.181)

page 8 (middle)
Unknown photographer
Portrait of John Forrest Explorer of Western Australia 1874
b&w photograph; 18.7 x 13.0 cm
National Library of Australia
Pictures Collection, nla.pic-an23382380

page 8 (bottom)
J. Macfarlane (active 1890–1898)
John Forrest's Party (His Brother, Alexander, Second in Command) Sight the Overland Telegraph Line, 1874 1890s
photoengraving; 52.5 x 69.0 cm
National Library of Australia
Pictures Collection, nla.pic-an9025855-6

page 9
Louis Haghe (1806–1885)
Portrait of Sir John Franklin 1840s
lithograph; 34.6 x 25.4 cm
National Library of Australia
Pictures Collection, nla.pic-an9579248

page 10 (top)

E. Forget

Nouvelle-Hollande, Baie des Chiens marins, camp de l'Uranie, sur la Presqu'ile Peron 1822?

hand-coloured engraving; 23.5 x 32.0 cm

National Library of Australia

Pictures Collection, nla.pic-an7567565

page 10 (bottom)

Alphonse Pellion

Baie des Chiens-marins, observatoire de l'Uranie 1927

colour collotype; 29.5 x 34.8 cm

National Library of Australia

Pictures Collection, nla.pic-an11510412

Chapter 2

page 12 (top)

J. Macfarlane (active 1890–1898)

Sturt's Party Threatened by Blacks at the Junction of the Murray and Darling, 1830 1890s

photoengraving; 52.5 x 69.0 cm

National Library of Australia

Pictures Collection, nla.pic-an9025855-1

page 12 (bottom)

J. Macfarlane (active 1890–1898)

Blacks About to Attack Leichardt's Camp, Near the Gulf of Carpentaria, 1845 1890s

photoengraving; 52.5 x 69.0 cm

National Library of Australia

Pictures Collection, nla.pic-an9025855-4

page 13

Ferdinand Jean Joubert (1810–1884)

Edward John Eyre, Lieut.-Governor of Jamaica, From a Painting in the Possession of the Family 1865

etching; 15.0 x 11.4 cm

National Library of Australia

Pictures Collection, nla.pic-an9455843

page 14 (top left)

Augustus Earle (1793–1838)

Remarkable Passage in the Cliffs, Port Jackson 1826?

watercolour; 24.4 x 11.4 cm

National Library of Australia

Pictures Collection, nla.pic-an2820731

page 14 (bottom)

Eugene Von Guérard (1811–1901)

Govetts Leap, the Blue Mountains (detail) 1872–1873

oil on board; 47.4 x 62.7 cm

National Library of Australia

Pictures Collection, nla.pic-an2272113

page 15

Denison Ranges, central Australia

Photo: Peter Macinnis

page 17 (top)

John Flynn (1880–1951)

Unidentifed Person Walking up Sand Dune, Innamincka, South Australia (between 1937 and 1942)

b&w glass negative; 8.2 x 10.7 cm

National Library of Australia

Pictures Collection, nla.pic-an24647823

page 17 (bottom)

Richard Woldendorp (b.1927)

Aerial View of Sand Dunes in the Strzelecki Desert, Northeast South Australia, 2000

colour photograph; 26.7 x 35.5 cm

National Library of Australia

Pictures Collection, nla.pic-vn3102337

Courtesy of Richard Woldendorp

page 17 (bottom, inset)

Unknown artist

Captain Charles Sturt 1895

wood engraving; 15.2 x 10.3 cm

National Library of Australia

Pictures Collection, nla.pic-an9941030

page 18 (top)

John Flynn (1880–1951)

Central Australian Desert Scene with Trees (detail) (between 1912 and 1951)

coloured lantern slide; 8.2 x 8.2 cm

National Library of Australia

Pictures Collection, nla.pic-an24652806

page 18 (middle)

Unknown photographer

Portrait of Ernest Giles, Australian Explorer (between 1860 and 1897)

b&w photograph; 10.5 x 7.9 cm

National Library of Australia

Pictures Collection, nla.pic-an24189206

page 18 (bottom)

Samuel Thomas Gill (1818–1880)

Country NW of Tableland, Aug. 22 (detail) c.1846

watercolour; 19.0 x 30.7 cm

National Library of Australia

Pictures Collection, nla.pic-an2376654

page 19 (top left)

Unknown artist

Camel Team in Flooded Country, South Australia 1913

postcard; 8.7 x 13.7 cm

National Library of Australia

Pictures Collection, nla.pic-an23217498

page 19 (top right, above)

John Flynn (1880–1951)

Camel Cart, Alice Springs (detail) (between 1912 and 1951)

b&w lantern slide; 8.2 x 8.2 cm

National Library of Australia

Pictures Collection, nla.pic-an24652817

page 19 (top right, below)

John Flynn (1880–1951)

Camel's Mouth (detail) 1926

hand-coloured lantern slide; 8.2 x 8.2 cm

National Library of Australia

Pictures Collection, nla.pic-an24527054

page 19 (bottom)

Unknown photographer

Dandenong State Forest, the Ferns in Fern Tree Gully, Victoria c.1880

b&w photograph; 14.0 x 19.0 cm

National Library of Australia

Pictures Collection, nla.pic-an10608594-38

page 20

Unknown artist

Adieu (detail)

reproduced from *Cassell's Picturesque Australasia*, vol. 3, edited by E.E. Morris

(London: Cassell & Company, Limited, 1890, p.188)

page 21 (top)

Paul Hardy

An Improvised Punt

reproduced from *Cassell's Picturesque Australasia*, vol. 3, edited by E.E. Morris

(London: Cassell & Company, Limited, 1890, p.176)

page 21 (middle)

J. Macfarlane (active 1890–1898)

Captain Rossiter Comes to Eyre's Aid, Great Australian Bight, 1841 1890s

photoengraving; 52.5 x 69.0 cm

National Library of Australia

Pictures Collection, nla.pic-an9025855-2

page 21 (below)

F.A. Sleap

Hume and Hovell Crossing the Murray in 1825 1880s

wood engraving; 18.1 x 14.8 cm

National Library of Australia

Pictures Collection, nla.pic-an8960228

page 23 (top)

Cairn on Mount Harris, 2006

Photo: Peter Macinnis

page 23 (bottom)

View of the Warrumbungle Range, 2006

Photo: Peter Macinnis

page 24

Unknown photographer

Portrait of Ernest Giles, Australian Explorer (detail) (between 1860 and 1897)

b&w photograph; 10.5 x 7.9 cm

National Library of Australia

Pictures Collection, nla.pic-an24189206

page 24 (background)

Eugene Von Guérard (1811–1901)

Mount Kosciusko, from the North-west (detail) 1867

hand-coloured lithograph; 32.5 x 51.0 cm

National Library of Australia

Pictures Collection, nla.pic-an7744695

page 25 (top)

J. Macfarlane (active 1890–1898)

John McDouall Stuart Planting the Union Jack on Central Mount Stuart, 1860 1890s

photoengraving; 52.5 x 69.0 cm

National Library of Australia

Pictures Collection, nla.pic-an9025855-5

page 25 (bottom)

Unknown artist

Sturt at Depot Creek (detail)

reproduced from *Cassell's Picturesque Australasia*, vol. 3, edited by E.E. Morris

(London: Cassell & Company, Limited, 1890, p.193)

page 26

Royal Society of Victoria

Yandruwandha Breastplate 1861

Image provided by the South Australian Museum, Adelaide, Australia, 2008

page 27

Unknown photographer

Tree in Queensland Marked by Leichhardt (detail) 1960s

b&w negative; 7.8 x 4.6 cm

National Library of Australia

Pictures Collection, nla.pic-vn3360295

page 27 (bottom)

Frank Clune (1893–1971)

Charles Sturt's Marked Tree, Sturt 1845, Cooper Creek, South Australia, 1935 (detail)

glass lantern slide; 8.3 cm x 8.0 cm

National Library of Australia

Pictures Collection, nla.pic-vn3506774

page 28
Hall & Co. Photo. Sydney
Marked Tree, Cooper's Creek, Burke and Wills' Expedition (detail) 1911?
b&w photograph; 40.6 x 56.7 cm
National Library of Australia
Pictures Collection, nla.pic-an23492483

Chapter 3

page 30
Samuel White Sweet (1825–1886)
Aboriginal Australian Weapons and Hunting Implements (detail) 1870s?
sepia photograph; 15.9 x 21.8 cm
National Library of Australia
Pictures Collection, nla.pic-vn3083070

page 31
Unknown photographer
Mrs Lores Bonney Overhauls Her Machine, a DH 60G Moth, My Little Ship, *VH-UPV, at Darwin on Arrival, 11 April, 1933*
b&w photograph; 9.1 x 12.9 cm
National Library of Australia
Pictures Collection, nla.pic-vn3723110

page 32 (left)
John Hunter (1737–1821)
Handsome Wedge Pea (Gompholobium grandiflorum) (detail) (between 1788 and 1790)
watercolour; 22.6 x 18.3 cm
National Library of Australia
Pictures Collection, nla.pic-an3149614

page 32 (right)
Ellis Rowan (1848–1922)
York Road Poison (Gastrolobium calycinum) 1900s
watercolour; 56.0 x 38.0 cm
National Library of Australia
Pictures Collection, nla.pic-an6632702

page 33 (top)
John Heaviside Clark (c.1770–1863), artist
M. Dubourg (active 1786–1808), engraver
Smoking Out the Opossum 1813
hand-coloured aquatint; 23.8 x 18.5 cm
National Library of Australia
Pictures Collection, nla.pic-an8936118

page 33 (middle)
Joseph Lycett (c.1775–1828)
Aborigines Using Fire to Hunt Kangaroos c.1817
watercolour; 17.7 x 27.8 cm
National Library of Australia
Pictures Collection, nla.pic-an2962715-s20

page 33 (bottom)
Unknown artist
Natives Pursuing Kangaroos in the Neighbourhood of Sydney, New South Wales 1820s
hand-coloured wood engraving; 5.6 x 21.0 cm
National Library of Australia
Pictures Collection, nla.pic-an7891507

page 34 (top)
Pandanus fruit
Photo: Peter Macinnis

page 34 (middle)
Cycad palm
Photo: Peter Macinnis

page 34 (bottom)
Unknown artist
Portrait of Ludwig Leichhardt c.1850
hand-coloured lithograph; 15.5 x 12.9 cm
National Library of Australia
Pictures Collection, nla.pic-an21971599

page 35
Edward Gilks (b.1822?)
from a photograph by Thomas Adams Hill (active 1856–1869)
William John Wills, Astronomer and Surveyor to the Victorian Exploration Expedition, Died at Coopers Creek About 2nd July, 1861
lithograph; 23.1 x 16.6 cm
National Library of Australia
Pictures Collection, nla.pic-an9869835

page 35 (background)
Jon Rhodes (b.1947)
Nardoo (Marsilea drummondii) (detail) 2001
b&w photograph; 8.7 x 23.7 cm
National Library of Australia
Pictures Collection, nla.pic-an23407404
Courtesy of Jon Rhodes

page 36 (left)
Edward Gilks (b.1822?)
from a photograph by Thomas Adams Hill (active 1856–1869)
William John Wills, Astronomer and Surveyor to the Victorian Exploration Expedition, Died at Coopers Creek About 2nd July, 1861
lithograph; 23.1 x 16.6 cm
National Library of Australia
Pictures Collection, nla.pic-an9869835

page 36 (right)
William Egley (1798–1870)
Portrait of Admiral J. Lort Stokes 1864
oil on photographic print; 27.7 x 22.6 cm
National Library of Australia
Pictures Collection, nla.pic-an4102905

page 36 (bottom right)

A.J. Mason

Killing a Kangaroo

reproduced from *Discoveries in Australia*, vol. 2, by John Lort Stokes

(London: T. and W. Boone, 1846, p.487)

page 37 (top)

Edward Roper (c.1830–1904)

Possum Shooting by Moonlight c.1855

oil on academy board; 19.0 x 12.2 cm

National Library of Australia

Pictures Collection, nla.pic-an2268342

page 37 (background)

Samuel Thomas Gill (1818–1880)

Aborigines and White Men Hunting Kangaroos (detail) c.1850

sepia wash drawing; 24.0 x 37.1 cm

National Library of Australia

Pictures Collection, nla.pic-an2377232

page 38 (top)

G. Gore

Killing an Alligator, Victoria River

reproduced from *Discoveries in Australia*, vol. 2, by John Lort Stokes

(London: T. and W. Boone, 1846, p.57)

page 38 (bottom)

Unknown artist

Australian Exploration, an Expedition on the March, Dec. 26, 1874

tinted wood engraving; 35.5 x 52.8 cm

National Library of Australia

Pictures Collection, nla.pic-an8960261

page 39

Unknown artist

Phillip Parker King

reproduced from *Cassell's Picturesque Australasia*, vol. 2, edited by E.E. Morris

(London: Cassell & Company, Limited, 1890)

Chapter 4

page 46

Sarah Stone (1760–1844)

Tabuan Parrot 1790

watercolour; 23.0 x 17.2 cm

National Library of Australia

Pictures Collection, nla.pic-an9063504

page 47 (top)

Unknown creator

Pair of Victorian Taxidermist Birds under a Glass Dome with Nest with Eggs and Butterfly

Courtesy of E.J. Ainger Pty Ltd

page 47 (bottom left)

Joseph Collyer (1748–1827)

Sir Joseph Banks, Bart., President of the Royal Society 1789

stipple engraving; oval image 10.4 x 8.1 cm

National Library of Australia

Pictures Collection, nla.pic-an9283208

page 47 (bottom right)

Unknown artist

Portrait of Cook (detail) 1800s

oil on canvas; 97.8 x 134.6 cm

National Library of Australia

Pictures Collection, nla.pic-an2291508

page 48 (top left)

Unknown engraver

after a painting by George Stubbs (1724–1806)

An Animal Found on the Coast of New Holland Called Kanguroo (i.e kangaroo) 1773

engraving; 23.0 x 26.5 cm

National Library of Australia

Pictures Collection, nla.pic-an7946248

page 48 (top right)

Peter Mazell

The Kangooroo (i.e. kangaroo) 1789

engraving; 28.3 x 21.7 cm

National Library of Australia

Pictures Collection, nla.pic-an9939754

page 48 (bottom)

Choubard (active 1807–1830)

Nouvelle-Hollande, Ile King, le Wombat 1807

hand-coloured engraving; 24.0 x 31.5 cm

National Library of Australia

Pictures Collection, nla.pic-an7573691

page 49 (left)

Kerry & Co.

Preserved Koalas, Mother and Child, on Display 1894

b&w photograph; 19.6 x 14.5 cm

National Library of Australia

Pictures Collection, nla.pic-an3366506-s82-b1

page 49 (right)

Unknown artist

Koala 1880s

colour engraving; 12.8 x 19.0 cm

National Library of Australia

Pictures Collection, nla.pic-an9939719-1

page 50 (background)

Kerry & Co.

Preserved Wallabies on Display (detail) 1894

b&w photograph; 15.0 x 20.0 cm

National Library of Australia

Pictures Collection, nla.pic-an3366506-s82-a2

page 50 (bottom)

Drawers of bird skins at Museum Victoria

Photo: Benjamin Healley

page 51 (top)

Choubard (active 1807–1830)

Nouvelle-Hollande, Nelle. Galles du Sud, Ornithorinque ... 1807

hand-coloured engraving; 24.2 x 31.8 cm

National Library of Australia

Pictures Collection, nla.pic-an7568602

page 51 (bottom left)

Thomas Baines (1820–1875)

Alligator on the Mud, Victoria River, June 1856

watercolour; 7.3 x 13.0 cm

National Library of Australia

Pictures Collection, nla.pic-an2679016

page 51 (bottom right)

Unknown artist

Description of the Alligator

reproduced from *Discoveries in Australia*, vol. 2, by John Lort Stokes

(London: T. and W. Boone, 1846, p.56)

page 52 (top)

Marrianne Collinson Campbell (1827–1903)

Orchard Swallowtail Butterfly (*Papilio aegeus aegeus*) 1840s

watercolour; 16.1 x 22.0 cm

National Library of Australia

Pictures Collection, nla.pic-vn3623649

page 52 (below)

Unknown artist

Spider, Slug and Praying Mantis 1842

watercolour; 23.7 x 17.3 cm

National Library of Australia

Pictures Collection, nla.pic-an6244852

page 53 (top left)

John William Lewin (1770–1819)

Sphinx ardenia (detail) 1805

hand-coloured engraving; 20.2 x 15.2 cm

National Library of Australia

Pictures Collection, nla.pic-an10493461

page 53 (top right)

John William Lewin (1770–1819)

Hepialus ligniveren (detail) 1805

hand-coloured engraving; 20.2 x 15.2 cm

National Library of Australia

Pictures Collection, nla.pic-an10493490

page 53 (bottom)

Marrianne Collinson Campbell (1827–1903)

Orchard Swallowtail Butterfly (*Papillio excellieus, i.e. Papilio aegeus aegeus*) 1840s

watercolour; 12.9 x 19.3 cm

National Library of Australia

Pictures Collection, nla.pic-vn3545852

Chapter 5

page 58

Unknown artist

View at the Encampment in Careening Bay, Where the Mermaid Was Repaired 1825

aquatint; 10.2 x 16.4 cm

National Library of Australia

Pictures Collection, nla.pic-an9537807

page 59 (top)

Derwentia derwentiana subsp. *derwentiana*

plant specimen collected in 1998

© Centre for Plant Biodiversity Research

page 59 (bottom)

Eucalyptus platyphylla

plant specimen collected by Joseph Banks and Daniel Solander in 1770

© Centre for Plant Biodiversity Research

page 59 (middle right)

Unknown artist

Portrait of Ludwig Leichhardt c.1850

hand-coloured lithograph; 15.5 x 12.9 cm

National Library of Australia

Pictures Collection, nla.pic-an21971599

page 60

William Byrne (1743–1805)

A View of Endeavour River, on the Coast of New Holland, Where the Ship Was Laid on Shore in Order to Repair the Damage Which She Received on the Rock 1773

engraving; 24.3 x 50.0 cm

National Library of Australia

Pictures Collection, nla.pic-an9184938

page 61

G.C. Fenton

Sturt Pea, Central Australia 1860s

watercolour; 12.8 x 17.5 cm

National Library of Australia

Pictures Collection, nla.pic-an5836959

page 62 (background)

Ida McComish (1885–1978)

Correa alba, Botany Bay, New South Wales (between 1936 and 1956)

watercolour; 8.6 x 6.9 cm

National Library of Australia

Pictures Collection, nla.pic-an24894821-s29-b2

page 62 (bottom)

Ebenezer Edward Gostelow (1867–1944)

Eremophila longifolia (*Emu Bush, Warrior Bush*), *Eremophila maculata* (*Native Fuchsia*) (detail) 1920

watercolour; 33.3 x 24.0 cm

National Library of Australia

Pictures Collection, nla.pic-an6135530

page 63 (top)

Glenys Ferguson (b.1943)

Beginning of Yarra Glen Leading to Woden Valley, in the Distance the Young Suburb of Curtin and in the Foreground the Yet-to-be-built Overpass to Government House and the Cotter Road, Canberra, c.1963

digital reproduction, 2006, of colour slide

National Library of Australia

Pictures Collection, nla.pic-vn3662409

Courtesy of Glenys Ferguson

page 63 (bottom left)

Unknown artist

Tomb of Allen (i.e. Allan) Cunningham Esqr. at Sydney 1840?

hand-coloured lithograph; 24.2 x 19.5 cm

National Library of Australia

Pictures Collection, nla.pic-an9224346

page 63 (bottom right)

Ida McComish (1885–1978)

Banksia ericifolia, *Botany Bay, New South Wales* (between 1936 and 1956)

watercolour; 20.2 x 26.5 cm

National Library of Australia

Pictures Collection, nla.pic-an24894821-s5-a2

Chapter 6

page 68

Journal of HM Bark *Endeavour*, 1768–1771

National Library of Australia

Manuscripts Collection, nla.gov.au/nla.ms-ms1

page 69

James Cook (1728–1779)

journal entry of 6 May 1770 (detail)

reproduced from the Journal of HM Bark *Endeavour*, 1768–1771

National Library of Australia

Manuscripts Collection, nla.gov.au/nla.ms-ms1

page 70

Samuel Atkins (active 1787–1808)

HMS Endeavour *off the Coast of New Holland* (detail) 1794?

watercolour; 38.0 x 50.8 cm

National Library of Australia

Pictures Collection, nla.pic-an5921609

page 70 (background)

James Cook (1728–1779)

journal entry of 11 June 1770 (detail)

reproduced from the Journal of HM Bark *Endeavour*, 1768–1771

National Library of Australia

Manuscripts Collection, nla.gov.au/nla.ms-ms1

page 71

Unknown artist

Portrait of John McDouall Stuart 1862?

mezzotint; 18.6 x 12.8 cm

National Library of Australia

Pictures Collection, nla.pic-an10038025

page 72 (left)

William John Wills (1834–1861)

journal entry of Thursday 30 May 1861

reproduced from *William John Wills' Journal of Trip 'from Cooper Creek towards Adelaide', 23 April 1861 – 26 June 1861*

National Library of Australia

Manuscripts Collection, nla.ms-ms30-7-s60

page 72 (left, inset)

Edward Gilks (b.1822?)

from a photograph by Thomas Adams Hill (active 1856–1869)

William John Wills, Astronomer and Surveyor to the Victorian Exploration Expedition, Died at Coopers Creek About 2nd July, 1861

lithograph; 23.1 x 16.6 cm

National Library of Australia

Pictures Collection, nla.pic-an9869835

page 72 (right)

Barcroft Capel Boake (1838–1921)

Portrait of William Carron, Died 25 February, 1876 1870s

b&w photograph; 10.0 x 5.6 cm

National Library of Australia

Pictures Collection, nla.pic-an24170767

page 73 (left)

Unknown photographer

Portrait of Ernest Giles, Australian Explorer (between 1860 and 1897)

b&w photograph; 10.5 x 7.9 cm

National Library of Australia

Pictures Collection, nla.pic-an24189206

page 73 (right)

Unknown artist

Portrait of John McDouall Stuart 1862?

mezzotint; 18.6 x 12.8 cm

National Library of Australia

Pictures Collection, nla.pic-an10038025

page 76 (top)

Unknown artist

Portrait of Ernest Giles, Australian Explorer (between 1860 and 1897)

b&w photograph; 10.5 x 7.9 cm

National Library of Australia

Pictures Collection, nla.pic-an24189206

page 76 (bottom left)

John Flynn (1880–1951)

Camel Train with Dog Sitting on Top of a Camel (detail) (between 1912 and 1955)

b&w lantern slide; 8.2 x 8.2 cm

National Library of Australia

Pictures Collection, nla.pic-an24353638

page 76 (bottom right)
William Romaine Govett (1807–1848)
Major Mitchell Sketching the Entrance of the Caves in Wellington Valley, New South Wales (detail) 1843
pen; 23.0 x 29.0 cm
National Library of Australia
Pictures Collection, nla.pic-an4700786

page 77 (left)
George Raper (1769–1796)
Common Bronzewing (Phaps chalcoptera) 1788?
watercolour, metallic paint; 45.8 x 30.2 cm
National Library of Australia
Pictures Collection, nla.pic-vn3579136

page 77 (right)
John Hunter (1737–1821)
Common Bronzewing (Phaps chalcoptera) *and Forest Grass Tree* (Xanthorrhoea media) (between 1788 and 1790)
watercolour; 22.6 x 18.3 cm
National Library of Australia
Pictures Collection, nla.pic-an3148903

Chapter 7

page 80
Dripstone filter, Cooma Cottage, Yass
Photo: Peter Macinnis

page 81 (top)
water filter
after design by Mrs George Campbell
in *Diary of Mrs George Campbell* c.1860–1870
National Library of Australia
Manuscripts Collection, nla.ms-ms840

page 81 (bottom left)
Unknown artist
Kangaroos and Cockatoos (detail) c.1880
chromolithograph; 17.7 x 26.3 cm
National Library of Australia
Pictures Collection, nla.pic-an23288896

page 81 (bottom right)
Ebenezer Edward Gostelow (1867–1944)
The Peaceful Dove (Geopelia placida); *the Diamond Dove* (Geopelia cuneata) 1934
watercolour; 51.0 x 38.4 cm
National Library of Australia
Pictures Collection, nla.pic-an3820248

page 82 (top)
Frederick Elliott (active 1855–1897)
Wa-Wee Waterhole 1891
b&w photograph
National Library of Australia
Pictures Collection, nla.pic-an6647833-14

page 82 (bottom)
Thomas Baines (1820–1875)
Party on Shore on Quail Island, Paterson's Bay, NW Coast, Australia 1855
pencil; 19.4 x 28.3 cm
National Library of Australia
Pictures Collection, nla.pic-an2678974

page 83
Unknown artist
Portrait of Ernest Giles, Australian Explorer (between 1860 and 1897)
b&w photograph; 10.5 x 7.9 cm
National Library of Australia
Pictures Collection, nla.pic-an24189206

page 84 (left)
Muddy water
Photo: Peter Macinnis

page 84 (top right)
Unknown artist
Portrait of John Oxley, 1783–1828, Explorer 1908
b&w negative; 9.3 x 7.6 cm
National Library of Australia
Pictures Collection, nla.pic-vn3509743

page 84 (bottom right)
Ernest Giles (1835–1897
The Stinking Pit
reproduced from *Australia Twice Traversed: The Romance of Exploration: Being a Narrative Compiled from the Journals of Five Exploring Expeditions into and through Central South Australia and Western Australia, from 1872 to 1876*, vol. 1, by Ernest Giles
(London: Sampson, Low, Marston, Searle & Rivington, 1889, p.227)

page 86 (top)
Waterbottle Used by Captain Charles Sturt 1820s
black glass bottle, fibre cover; height 31.0 cm
National Library of Australia
Pictures Collection, nla.pic-an6393462

page 86 (bottom)
Samuel Thomas Gill (1818–1880)
Camp in Desert, Sept. 1st c.1846
watercolour; 19.0 x 30.6 cm
National Library of Australia
Pictures Collection, nla.pic-an2377306

page 87
Unknown photographer
Afghan Man Pouring Water from Bag into Cup (detail) (between 1912 and 1920)
sepia-toned photograph; 13.9 x 8.7 cm
National Library of Australia
Pictures Collection, nla.pic-vn3085332

page 88 (top left)
Unknown artist
The Underground Room
reproduced from *Cassell's Picturesque Australasia*, vol. 3, edited by E.E. Morris
(London: Cassell & Company, Limited, 1890, p.196)

page 88 (top right)
Unknown artist
Captain Charles Sturt 1895
wood engraving; 15.2 x 10.3 cm
National Library of Australia
Pictures Collection, nla.pic-an9941030

page 88 (bottom)
Percy Leason (1889–1959)
The Sturt Expedition Out of Food and Water 1916
oil on canvas; 100.0 x 151.7 cm
National Library of Australia
Pictures Collection, nla.pic-an2268338
Courtesy of Max Leason

page 89
Michael Jensen (b.1943)
Frank Woerle Taking a Shower at Cannon Hill Ranger Station, Northern Territory, 1973
b&w photograph; 26.8 x 38.8 cm
National Library of Australia
Pictures Collection, nla.pic-vn3550857
Courtesy of Michael Jensen

page 89 (background)
Francis Reiss (b.1927)
View of the Tanami Desert, in the Area Known as the Pound, Balgo Hills, 2003 (detail)
colour digital photograph
National Library of Australia
Pictures Collection, nla.pic-vn3294966
Courtesy of Francis Reiss

page 90
George Hamilton (1812–1883)
Bushmen Watering Horses in the Desert of Australia c.1840
hand-coloured lithograph; 27.6 x 38.6 cm
National Library of Australia
Pictures Collection, nla.pic-an5576862

Chapter 8

page 94
Unknown photographer
Francis Birtles on His Bicycle (between 1899 and 1928?)
b&w photograph; 14.3 x 8.6 cm
National Library of Australia
Pictures Collection, nla.pic-vn3303106

page 95 (top)
Unknown photographer
An Aboriginal Mechanic Using the Sap of the Bloodwood Tree and a Hot Stick to Repair the Oldsmobile 30, Arnhem Land (between 1899 and 1928?)
b&w photograph; 8.5 x 14.2 cm
National Library of Australia
Pictures Collection, nla.pic-vn3301757

page 95 (middle)
Unknown artist
Portrait of John McDouall Stuart 1862?
mezzotint; 18.6 x 12.8 cm
National Library of Australia
Pictures Collection, nla.pic-an10038025

page 95 (bottom)
Unknown artist
Last Moments of Wills the Australian Explorer 1860s
engraving; 17.7 cm x 22.7 cm
National Library of Australia
Pictures Collection, nla.pic-an8960252

page 96 (top)
Unknown photographer
Portrait of Ernest Giles, Australian Explorer (between 1860 and 1897)
b&w photograph; 10.5 x 7.9 cm
National Library of Australia
Pictures Collection, nla.pic-an24189206

page 96 (bottom left)
Ernest Giles (1835–1897
Dragged by Diaway (detail)
reproduced from *Australia Twice Traversed: The Romance of Exploration: Being a Narrative Compiled from the Journals of Five Exploring Expeditions into and through Central South Australia and Western Australia, from 1872 to 1876*, vol. 1, by Ernest Giles
(London: Sampson, Low, Marston, Searle & Rivington, 1889, p.295)

page 96 (bottom right)
Ernest Giles (1835–1897
An Accident in Camp (detail)
reproduced from *Australia Twice Traversed: The Romance of Exploration: Being a Narrative Compiled from the Journals of Five Exploring Expeditions into and through Central South Australia and Western Australia, from 1872 to 1876*, vol. 1, by Ernest Giles
(London: Sampson, Low, Marston, Searle & Rivington, 1889, p.147)

page 97 (top)
Frank Hurley (1885–1962)
Crocodile Lying in Shallow Water (detail) (between 1910 and 1962)
b&w glass negative; 12.0 x 16.3 cm
National Library of Australia
Pictures Collection, nla.pic-an23378093
Courtesy of the Estate of Frank Hurley

page 97 (bottom)

Geoffrey Chapman Ingleton (1908–1998)

H.M. Bark Endeavour 1937

sepia etching; 22.5 x 28.5 cm

National Library of Australia

Pictures Collection, nla.pic-an6152165

Courtesy of the estate of Geoffrey Chapman

Ingleton**page 98**

William Egley (1798–1870)

Portrait of Admiral J. Lort Stokes 1864

oil on photographic print; 27.7 x 22.6 cm

National Library of Australia

Pictures Collection, nla.pic-an4102905

page 99 (top)

Montagu Scott (1835–1909)

The Finding of King, the Survivor 1865

wood engraving; 10.7 x 27.0 cm

National Library of Australia

Pictures Collection, nla.pic-an8960194

page 99 (bottom left)

Nicholas Chevalier (1828–1902)

Return of Burke and Wills to Coopers Creek
(detail) 1868

oil on canvas; 89.2 x 120.0 cm

National Library of Australia

Pictures Collection, nla.pic-an2265463

page 99 (bottom right)

Thomas Baines (1820–1875)

*Mr. Gregory's Horse Treads on an Alligator in
Fording Victoria River, April, 1856* (detail)

watercolour; 7.3 x 13.0 cm

National Library of Australia

Pictures Collection, nla.pic-an2680779

page 100

Ignaz Sebastian Klauber (1753–1817)

*Gezigt van de Rivier Endeavour op de Kust van
Nieuw-Holland* (detail) 1795

engraving; 21.5 x 35.2 cm

National Library of Australia

Pictures Collection, nla.pic-an9193430

page 101 (top)

Unknown artist

Burial of Burke by Howitt's Party

reproduced from *Cassell's Picturesque Australasia*,
vol. 3, edited by E.E. Morris

(London: Cassell & Company, Limited, 1890,
p.293)

page 101 (bottom left)

Unknown artist

Portrait of Ludwig Leichhardt c.1850

hand-coloured lithograph; 15.5 x 12.9 cm

National Library of Australia

Pictures Collection, nla.pic-an21971599

page 101 (bottom right)

William Strutt (1825–1915)

Cooey (detail) c.1876

pen; 25.0 x 21.8 cm

National Library of Australia

Pictures Collection, nla.pic-an3241500

pages 102–103

Richard Bridges Beechey (1808–1895)

*Lt. J. Stokes Speared in the Lungs While
Discovering the Victoria River, Australia, 1839*
1863

oil on canvas; 64.6 x 91.6 cm

National Library of Australia

Pictures Collection, nla.pic-an2291837

Chapter 9

page 106

Arthur Groom (1904–1953)

*With Rising Wind a Centralian Desert Storm is
About to Break, Northern Territory, 1947*

b&w photograph; 15.6 x 20.7 cm

National Library of Australia

Pictures Collection, nla.pic-vn3078635

page 107 (top)

John Oxley (1783–1828)

A Chart of Part of the Interior of New South Wales
(detail) 1822

coloured map, dissected and mounted on linen;
63.1 x 94.2 cm

National Library of Australia

Maps Collection, nla.map-t939

page 107 (bottom)

Unknown photographer

Portrait of John Oxley, 1783–1828, Explorer
(detail) 1908

b&w negative; 9.3 x 7.6 cm

National Library of Australia

Pictures Collection, nla.pic-vn3509743

page 108 (top)

Samuel Calvert (1828–1913)

*The Departure of the Leichhardt Search Expedition
from Glengower, from a Sketch by Francis H.
Nixon* (detail) 1865

wood engraving; 37.0 x 22.3 cm

National Library of Australia

Pictures Collection, nla.pic-an9025865

page 108 (bottom)

Archibald James Campbell (1853–1929)

*Four Unidentified Men, with Five Horses and a
Cart Crossing the Back Waters of the Flooded
River Red Gum Forest, 1894* (detail)

sepia-toned photograph; 9.2 x 14.5 cm

National Library of Australia

Pictures Collection, nla.pic-an24750370

page 109 (top)

Jeff Cutting (b.1945)

A Wall of Smoke Rising to the West of the Brindabella Ranges is from Strong Burning on the Broken Cart Fire in Kosciuszko National Park, Friday 17th January 2003

colour photograph; 25.6 x 39.5 cm

National Library of Australia

Pictures Collection, nla.pic-vn3510482

Courtesy of Jeff Cutting

page 109 (bottom)

Walter Jenner (1836–1902)

Shipwreck on Friday Island, Torres Strait (detail) 1881

oil on canvas; 25.6 x 46.2 cm

National Library of Australia

Pictures Collection, nla.pic-an2265534

page 111

John Flynn (1880–1951)

Unidentified Indigenous Man Shows Two Unidentified People How the Dry Mud Has Cracked (detail) (between 1912 and 1955)

coloured lantern slide; 8.2 x 8.2 cm

National Library of Australia

Pictures Collection, nla.pic-an24190291

page 112 (top)

Edward Gilks (b.1822?)

from a photograph by Thomas Adams Hill (active 1856–1869)

William John Wills, Astronomer and Surveyor to the Victorian Exploration Expedition, Died at Coopers Creek about 2nd July, 1861

lithograph; 23.1 x 16.6 cm

National Library of Australia

Pictures Collection, nla.pic-an9869835

page 112 (bottom)

Unknown artist

Watkin Tench

taken from a copy held in the Mitchell Library, State Library of New South Wales

pages 112–113

Sir Lionel Lindsay (1874–1961)

Study for Burden of the Heat of the Day 1920s

pen and ink and wash; 16.3 x 22.9 cm

National Library of Australia

Pictures Collection, nla.pic-an6631608

Chapter 10

page 116 (top)

Unknown artist

Leichardt (i.e. Leichhardt) *from a Portrait Taken by One of the Explorists from Moreton Bay to Swan River* 1846?

pencil; 17.5 x 12.2 cm

National Library of Australia

Pictures Collection, nla.pic-an6054888

page 116 (middle)

Alexander Denistoun

An Exploring Party Looking for a Sheep Run 1847

hand-coloured lithograph; 22.0 x 27.4 cm

National Library of Australia

Pictures Collection, nla.pic-an6016175

page 116 (bottom)

Victor Pillement (1767–1814)

Nouvelle-Hollande, Nouvelle Galles du Sud, vue de la Partie Meridionale de la Ville de Sydney, Capitale des Colonies Anglaises aux Terres Australes et de L'embouchure de la Riviere de Parramatta 1803 (detail) 1807

engraving; 24.0 x 49.0 cm

National Library of Australia

Pictures Collection, nla.pic-an7568621

page 117 (top)

Samuel Thomas Gill (1818–1880)

Bushman's Night Camp (detail) 1854?

hand-coloured lithograph; 12.0 x 19.0 cm

National Library of Australia

Pictures Collection, nla.pic-an7150056

page 117 (bottom)

John Pye (1782–1874), engraver

after William Westall (1781–1850), painter

View of Wreck-Reef Bank, Taken at Low Water (detail) 1814

engraving; 30.0 x 24.2 cm

National Library of Australia

Pictures Collection, nla.pic-an7746523

page 118 (left)

Unknown photographer

Dr Thomas Braidwood Wilson

reproduced from *'Back to Braidwood' Celebrations, 22nd November to 29th November 1925*

(Sydney: The Direct Publicity Co. under the auspices of the 'Back to Braidwood' Executive Committee, 1925)

page 118 (top right)

David Herrgott (1823–1861)

'The Explorer' Commencing His Dispatch. Bush Tent and Cradle of the Explorer Constructed on Scientific Principles (detail) 1858

pen and ink; approx. 8.5 x 14.5 cm

Courtesy of Royal Geographical Society of South Australia; SRGS MS 54c

page 118 (bottom right)

John Flynn (1880–1951)

Flies Covering a Pack on the Back of a Horse (detail) (between 1912 and 1955)

b&w lantern slide; 8.2 x 8.2 cm

National Library of Australia

Pictures Collection, nla.pic-an24397461

page 121

Samuel Thomas Gill (1818–1880)

Mt. Brown from Camp Looking NNE., Augst. 20th (detail) c.1846

watercolour; 18.0 x 31.2 cm

National Library of Australia

Pictures Collection, nla.pic-an2377303

page 122
S.T. Gill (1818–1880)
Invalid's Tent, Salt Lake 75 Miles North-west of Mount Arden 1846
watercolour on paper; 21.4 x 34.2 cm
Morgan Thomas Bequest Fund 1944
Art Gallery of South Australia, Adelaide, 0.1253

page 124 (top)
Unknown photographer
A Man Sitting Next to a Campfire with a Tarpaulin Erected Over a Car, Alligator River, Northern Territory (between 1899 and 1928)
b&w photograph; 8.3 x 13.2 cm
National Library of Australia
Pictures Collection, nla.pic-vn3302164

page 124 (middle)
Unknown photographer
Francis Birtles and His Bicycle Next to His Tent, Queensland (between 1899 and 1928?)
b&w photograph; 6.0 x 8.3 cm
National Library of Australia
Pictures Collection, nla.pic-vn3302402

page 124 (bottom)
Camel at sunset
Photo: Peter Macinnis

Chapter 11

page 126
Unknown artist
Watkin Tench
taken from a copy held in the Mitchell Library, State Library of New South Wales

page 128 (left)
Harold John Graham (1858–1929)
Heaving the Log. Stop! 1881
pen and ink; 9.0 x 20.1 cm
National Library of Australia
Pictures Collection, nla.pic-an6442355

page 128 (right)
A surveyor's chain, c.1860
Morpeth Museum, Morpeth, New South Wales
Photo: Peter Macinnis

page 128 (bottom)
Samuel Thomas Gill (1818–1880)
The Sandy Ridges of Central Australia (detail) c.1846
watercolour; 15.2 x 22.9 cm
National Library of Australia
Pictures Collection, nla.pic-an2377285

page 129 (top)
Unknown artist
Allan Cunningham, Botanist, Born July 1791 Died June 1839 1870s
lithograph; 43.6 x 33.7 cm
National Library of Australia
Pictures Collection, nla.pic-an9353072

page 129 (bottom left)
River Lett Hill, Blue Mountains, New South Wales
Photo: Peter Macinnis

page 129 (bottom right)
Lett River, Blue Mountains, New South Wales
Photo: Peter Macinnis

page 131 (top)
Map and GPS unit
Photo: Michael Stenning

page 131 (bottom left)
Surveyor's flat steel tape
Courtesy of Queensland Government Department of Natural Resources and Water

page 131 (bottom right)
Surveyor's perambulator
Courtesy of Queensland Government Department of Natural Resources and Water

page 133
Unknown artist
Lady Nelson 1870s
watercolour; 19.3 x 27.6 cm
National Library of Australia
Pictures Collection, nla.pic-an5943237

Chapter 12

page 137 (top left)
Gerard van Keulen
T Zuijd Land Ontdeckt Door Willem de Vlamingh in de Maande van Jan an Febrii 1697 Met t Yagt de Geelvink de Hooker de Nyptang ent Galjoot 't Weseltje (detail) 1697–1726
National Library of Australia
Maps Collection, nla.map-rm752

page 137 (bottom left)
Great Britain. Hydrographic Dept
Swan River and Rottnest Island (detail) 1845
National Library of Australia
Maps Collection, nla.map-t34

page 137 (right)
Abel Janszoon Tazman (1603?–1659)
Tasman's Manuscript of His Discovery of Australia (detail) 1895
National Library of Australia
Maps Collection, map-rm2056-2

page 138 (top)

Unknown artist

Entrance of Oyster Harbour, King George III Sound, Interview with the Natives 1825

aquatint; 12.5 x 17.8 cm

National Library of Australia

Pictures Collection, nla.pic-an7748236

page 138 (middle)

Charles Whitmore Babbage (b.1841)

Junction of the Rivers Marray & Darling, April 1860

pen and ink; 10.0 x 16.0 cm

National Library of Australia

Pictures Collection, nla.pic-vn3425980

page 138 (bottom)

Phillip Parker King (1791–1856)

Descarte (i.e. Descartes) Island One of the Institute (i.e. Insitut) Islands of Capt. Baudin 1820

watercolour; 8.5 x 11.5 cm

National Library of Australia

Pictures Collection, nla.pic-an6570381

page 139 (top)

Unknown maker

Compass Used by David Lindsay during His Explorations 1879

compass: bronze; diam. 4.1 cm

National Library of Australia

Pictures Collection, nla.pic-an7905973

page 139 (middle)

Unknown maker

Table of Star Signs and Dates, Compass, Spirit Level, Sundial, Astrolabe and Measuring Instrument in a Wooden Box 1750?

set of instruments: wood, bronze and glass; box size 3.3 x 43.7 x 9.9 cm

National Library of Australia

Pictures Collection, nla.pic-an7905959

page 139 (bottom)

C. Essex & Co., London

Compass, Sundial and Geographical Clock c.1780

compass: brass and wood; diam. 7.0 cm

National Library of Australia

Pictures Collection, nla.pic-an6561322

page 140 (background)

Augustin Legrand

Planisphere suivant la projection de Mercator, elemens de geographie moderne a l'usage des colleges et maisons d'education (detail) 1830?

colour map; 22.0 x 35.5 cm

National Library of Australia

Maps Collection, nla.map-rm3407

page 141 (top)

The 'Horizontal Waterfall', north of Broome, Western Australia, 2007

Photo: Peter Macinnis

page 141 (bottom)

Thomas Baines (1820–1875)

Tom Tough Ashore near Curiosity Peak, October 1856

watercolour; 7.3 x 12.9 cm

National Library of Australia

Pictures Collection, nla.pic-an2679012

page 142

Oswald Walters B. Brierly (1817–1894)

H.M.S. Rattlesnake *& Bramble* Tender Commanded by Captain Owen Stanley R.N, Finding an Entrance Through the Reefs into the Louisiade Archipelago, S.E. Extreme, New Guinea, June 14th, 1849 (detail) 1852

colour lithograph; 25.4 x 35.5 cm

National Library of Australia

Pictures Collection, nla.pic-an11905521

page 143 (top)

'First Map of Australia' from Nicholas Vallard's Atlas, 1547, in the Library of Sir Thomas Phillipps, Bart. at Middle Hill, 1856 (detail) 1856

facsimile of chart from Nicholas Vallard's manuscript sea atlas (1547), now held in the Huntington Library, San Marino, California

colour map; 37.6 x 55.4 cm

National Library of Australia

Maps Collection, nla.map-rm1819

page 143 (bottom)

Unknown artist

Portrait of John MacGillivray 1937

b&w picture; 13.3 x 13.3 cm

National Library of Australia

Pictures Collection, nla.pic-vn3793138

page 144

Walter Burley Griffin (1876–1937)

Exterior Views of Castlecrag Houses and Surveyor with Theodolite in Foreground (detail) (between 1920 and 1923)

b&w glass negative; 12.0 x 16.4 cm

National Library of Australia

Pictures Collection, nla.pic-vn3943114

pages 144–145 (bottom)

William Westall (1781–1850)

Views on the South Coast of Terra Australis. Plate XVII (detail) 1814

72.4 x 99.8 cm

National Library of Australia

Maps Collection, nla.map-t1573

page 145 (right)

George Raper (1769–1796)

Van Diemans Land, New Holland; The Land about Botany Bay; Entrance of Port Jackson When Close under the South Head 1791

ink and watercolour on paper; 23.2 x 18.5 cm

National Library of Australia

Maps Collection, nla.pic-an21511990

page 146 (left)

Hamilton Hume (1797–1873)

Mr Hume's Sketch of a Tour Performed by W.H. Hovell and Himself from Lake George to Port Phillip, Bass's Straits (detail) 1825

44.5 x 55.6 cm

National Library of Australia

Maps Collection, nla.map-f3

page 146 (right)

Unknown photographer

Portrait of Ernest Giles, Australian Explorer (between 1860 and 1897)

b&w photograph; 10.5 x 7.9 cm

National Library of Australia

Pictures Collection, nla.pic-an24189206

page 147

Dennis Adams (1914–2001)

Endeavour, below Decks 1970?

offset photomechanical print; 86.3 x 50.0 cm

National Library of Australia

Pictures Collection, nla.pic-an9537993

Courtesy of the executor of the Estate of Denis Adams

page 148

John Oxley (1783–1828)

A Chart of Part of the Interior of New South Wales (detail) 1822

63.1 x 94.2 cm

National Library of Australia

Maps Collection, nla.map-t939

Chapter 13

pages 154–155 (bottom)

Frank Hurley (1885–1962)

A Ploughed Field and a River, and beyond, Three Large and Several Smaller Pyramids, Cairo, Egypt (detail) (between 1939 and 1945)

plastic negative; 8.0 x 11.0 cm

National Library of Australia

Pictures Collection, nla.pic-an23564920

Courtesy of the Estate of Frank Hurley

page 155

William Hughes (1817–1876)

Australia 1866

colour map; 21.4 x 27.1 cm

National Library of Australia

Maps Collection, nla.map-t738

page 157

Near the Denison Ranges, South Australia

Photo: Peter Macinnis

page 158 (top)

John Harrison (1693–1776)

Marine Timekeeper (H1) 1735

brass, bronze, steel, oak, lignum vitae; height 67.3 cm

Courtesy of National Maritime Museum, Greenwich, London, Ministry of Defence Art Collection; D6783_3

page 158 (bottom left)

Harold John Graham (1858–1929)

Shooting the Sun (detail) 1881

watercolour, pen and ink; 5.0 x 7.6 cm

National Library of Australia

Pictures Collection, nla.pic-an6442463

page 158 (bottom right)

R.B. Bate (Firm)

Surveying Instruments Used by Sir Thomas Mitchell during His Three Expeditions 1831–1846

National Library of Australia

Pictures Collection, nla.pic-an6393476-1-s1

page 159

Unknown photographer

Photograph of the Moon Taken with the Great Melbourne Telescope, Moon's Age 9 Days 0 Hours 1880s

b&w photograph; 24.4 x 20.1 cm

National Library of Australia

Pictures Collection, nla.pic-an24599057

Chapter 14

page 162 (left)

M.L.W. (Bill) White

Duyfken 1960s

b&w print; 18.5 x 20.0 cm

National Library of Australia

Pictures Collection, nla.pic-vn3267997

page 162 (right)

Perth Mint (Western Australia)

Australia on the Map 1606–2006 c.2006

silver coin; diam. 4 cm

National Library of Australia

Pictures Collection, nla.pic-vn3987971

Courtesy of the Perth Mint

page 163

William Bentley (1836–1910)

Mt. Alexander Gold Diggings, 1853

watercolour; 23.0 x 35.3 cm

National Library of Australia

Pictures Collection, nla.pic-an6617924

page 164

Peter Hill

*View of the Central Murray Canyons Looking
Towards Kangaroo Island and the South
Australian Mainland …* 2005

reproduced from 'Geomorphology and Evolution
of the Gigantic Murray Canyons on the Australian
Southern Margin' by P.J. Hill, P. De Deckker and
N.F. Exon, *Australian Journal of Earth Sciences*,
vol. 52, 2005

Reprinted by permission of the publisher (Taylor &
Francis Ltd, www.informaworld.com)

page 165 (top left)

Frederic Whiting

Portrait of Dr G.E. Morrison 1902

watercolour; 48.5 x 39.5 cm

National Library of Australia

Pictures Collection, nla.pic-an6054853

page 165 (right)

Unknown photographer

Portrait of Francis Birtles in Arnhem Land
(between 1899 and 1928)

b&w photograph; 14.3 x 8.6 cm

National Library of Australia

Pictures Collection, nla.pic-vn3301801

page 165 (bottom)

Unknown photographer

*Francis Birtles and His Dog Camped beside the Car
Having a Drink, Arnhem Land* (detail) (between
1899 and 1928)

b&w photograph; 8.3 x 13.5 cm

National Library of Australia

Pictures Collection, nla.pic-vn3301921

page 166 (bottom)

Unknown photographer

*Mrs Dolores Bonney First Lady to Fly from
Australia to England* 1933

b&w photograph

National Library of Australia

Pictures Collection

page 167

Greg Power

*Lincoln Hall Portrait during His Visit and Talk at
the NLA, 22 Sep 07*

digital image

National Library of Australia

All National Library images are available
online. To find an image, go to www.nla.gov.au
and type the image number in the search box.

The images of the damper, the quill pen and
inkpot, and the nib on pages 42, 67 and 69
were taken by Gunther Glesti of the National
Library of Australia. The image of the excavator
on page 63 was taken by Tina Mattei of the
National Library of Australia. The images
of the frog, the water drops, the stars, the
wood panels and the canoeist on pages 113,
120, 132, 138 and 162 were sourced from
iStockphoto (www.istockphoto.com).

List of references for quotes

Chapter 1

page 4

Paul G. Fidlon (ed.), *The Journal of Philip Gidley King: Lieutenant, R.N. 1787–1790*. Sydney: Australian Documents Library, 1980, p.36.

page 9

Lady Franklin on the Gordon River, to her sister, April 1842 in Sir John and Lady Franklin, *Some Private Correspondence of Sir John and Lady Jane Franklin*. Dubbo: Review Publications Pty Ltd, 1977 (reprint of *Australian Historical Monographs*, Volume XV), Part II, p.48).

Chapter 2

page 13

Edward John Eyre, *Journals of Expeditions of Discovery into Central Australia and Overland from Adelaide to King George's Sound, in the years 1840–1; Sent by the Colonists of South Australia with the Sanction and Support of the Government: Including an Account of the Manners and Customs of the Aborigines and the State of Their Relations with Europeans*, vol. 1. London: T. and W. Boone, 1845, pp.167–168.

page 17

Charles Sturt, *Narrative of an Expedition into Central Australia, Performed Under the Authority of Her Majesty's Government, during the Years 1844, 5, and 6, Together with a Notice of the Province of South Australia, in 1847*, vol. 1. London: T. and W. Boone, 1849, pp.370–371.

page 18

Ernest Giles, *Australia Twice Traversed: The Romance of Exploration, Being a Narrative Compiled from the Journals of Five Exploring Expeditions into and through Central South Australia, and Western Australia, from 1872 to 1876*, vol. 2. London: Sampson, Low, Marston, Searle & Rivington, 1889, p.108.

page 24

Ernest Giles, *Australia Twice Traversed …*, vol. 1, pp.169–170.

Chapter 3

page 34

Ludwig Leichhardt, *Journal of an Overland Expedition in Australia, from Moreton Bay to Port Essington, a Distance of Upwards of 3000 Miles, during the Years 1844–1845*. London: T. and W. Boone, 1847, p.400.

page 36

William Wills (ed.), *A Successful Exploration through the Interior of Australia, from Melbourne to the Gulf of Carpentaria. From the Journals and Letters of William John Wills*. London: Richard Bentley, 1863, pp.291–292.

Chapter 4

page 47

Joseph D. Hooker (ed.), *Journal of the Right Hon. Sir Joseph Banks Bart., K.B., P.R.S. during Captain Cook's First Voyage in H.M.S. Endeavour in 1768–71 to Terra del Fuego, Otahite, New Zealand, Australia, the Dutch East Indies, etc.* London: MacMillan and Co. Ltd, 1896, p.287.

W.J.L. Wharton (ed.), *Captain Cook's Journal during his First Voyage Round the World Made in H.M.Bark 'Endeavour' in 1768–71*. London: Elliot Stock, 1893, p.294.

Chapter 5

page 59

Ludwig Leichhardt, *Journal of an Overland Expedition in Australia …*, p.417.

Chapter 6

page 70

James Cook, Journal of HMB *Endeavour*. National Library of Australia, Manuscripts Collection, MS 1. Available at nla.gov.au/nla.ms-ms1.

Joseph D. Hooker (ed.), *Journal of the Right Hon. Sir Joseph Banks Bart., K.B., P.R.S. during Captain Cook's First Voyage in H.M.S. Endeavour in 1768–71 to Terra del Fuego, Otahite, New Zealand, Australia, the Dutch East Indies, etc.* London: MacMillan and Co. Ltd, 1896.

page 71

William Hardman (ed.), *Explorations in Australia. The Journals of John McDouall Stuart during the Years 1858, 1859, 1860, 1861, & 1862, When He Fixed the Centre of the Continent and Successfully Crossed It from Sea to Sea*. London: Saunders, Otley, and Co., 1865, p.52.

Ida Lee (ed.), *The Logbook of the 'Lady Nelson' with the Journal of Her First Commander Lieutenant James Grant, R.N.* London: Grafton & Co., 1915, p.147.

page 72

William John Wills, *The Diary of William John Wills: 23 April – 28 June 1861*. National Library of Australia, Manuscripts Collection, MS 30/7. Available at www.nla.gov.au/epubs/wills/.

William Carron, *Narrative of an Expedition Undertaken Under the Direction of the Late Mr. Assistant Surveyor E.B. Kennedy, for the Exploration of the Country Lying between Rockingham Bay and Cape York*. Sydney: Kemp and Fairfax, 1849, p.78.

page 73

Ernest Giles, *Australia Twice Traversed …*, vol. 2, pp.220–221.

William Hardman (ed.), *Explorations in Australia …*, p.438.

page 76

Ernest Giles, *Australia Twice Traversed …*, vol. 2, pp.261.

Chapter 7

page 83

Ernest Giles, *Australia Twice Traversed …*, vol. 2, pp.169–170.

page 84

John Oxley, *Journals of Two Expeditions into the Interior of New South Wales, Undertaken by Order of the British Government in the Years 1817–18.* London: John Murray, 1820, p.156.

page 88

Charles Sturt, *Narrative of an Expedition into Central Australia …*, pp.305–306.

Chapter 8

page 95

William Hardman (ed.), *Explorations in Australia …*, p.221 [sic, p.321].

page 96

Ernest Giles, *Australia Twice Traversed …*, vol. 1, p.233.

page 98

J. Lort Stokes, *Discoveries in Australia; with an Account of the Coasts and Rivers Explored and Surveyed during the Voyage of H.M.S.* Beagle, *in the Years 1837–38–39–40–41–42–43. By Command of the Lords Commissioners of the Admiralty. And also a Narrative of Captain Owen Stanley's Visits to the Islands in the Araf ra Sea,* vol. 2. London: T. and W. Boone, 1846, p.37.

page 101

Ludwig Leichhardt, *Journal of an Overland Expedition in Australia …*, p.65.

Chapter 9

page 107

John Oxley, *Journals of Two Expeditions into the Interior of New South Wale …*, p.116.

page 112

Watkin Tench, *A Complete Account of the Settlement at Port Jackson, Including an Accurate Description of the Situation of the Colony; of the Natives; and of Its Natural Productions; Taken on the Spot, by Captain Watkin Tench, of the Marines.* London: G. Nicol, J. Sewell, 1793, p.131.

William Wills (ed.), *A Successful Exploration through the Interior of Australia …*, pp.145–146.

Chapter 10

page 118

T.B. Wilson, *Narrative of a Voyage Round the World; Comprehending an Account of the Wreck of the Ship 'Governor Ready', in Torres Straits; a Description of the British Settlements on the Coasts of New Holland, More Particularly Raffles Bay, Melville Island, Swan River, and King George's Sound; also, The Manners and Customs of the Aboriginal Tribes; with an Appendix, Containing Remarks on Transportation, the Treatment of Convicts during the Voyage, and Advice to Persons Intending To Emigrate to the Australian Colonies.* London: Dawson's, 1968 (1835 first edition), p.247.

Chapter 11

page 126

Watkin Tench, *A Complete Account of the Settlement at Port Jackson …*, pp.113–114.

page 129

Ida Lee, *Early Explorers in Australia from the Log-Books and Journals, Including the Diary of Allan Cunningham, Botanist, from March 1, 1817, to November 19, 1818.* London: Methuen & Co. Ltd., 1925, p.214.

page 133

F.M. Bladen (ed.), *Historical Records of New South Wales*, vol. 4—Hunter and King. 1800, 1801, 1802. Sydney: Charles Potter, Government Printer, 1896, p.483.

Chapter 12

page 143

John MacGillivray, *Narrative of The Voyage of H.M.S.* Rattlesnake, *Commanded by the Late Captain Owen Stanley, R.N., F.R.S. &c. during the Years 1846–1850. Including Discoveries and Surveys in New Guinea, the Louisiade Archipelago, etc., To Which Is Added the Account of Mr. E.B. Kennedy's Expedition for the Exploration of the Cape York Peninsula,* vol. 1. London: published under the Sanction of the Lords Commissioners of the Admiralty, T. & W. Boone, 1852, p.84.

page 146

Ernest Giles, *Australia Twice Traversed …*, vol. 2, p.330.

Chapter 13

page 156

J. Bronowski, *The Ascent of Man.* London: British Broadcasting Corporation, 1973, p.127.

Index

Page numbers in **bold** refer to illustrations.